Enabling Lightweight Real-time Collaboration

INFORMATIONSTECHNOLOGIE UND ÖKONOMIE
Herausgegeben von Christian Becker, Wolfgang Gaul,
Armin Heinzl, Martin Schader und Daniel Veit

Band 48

PETER LANG
Frankfurt am Main · Berlin · Bern · Bruxelles · New York · Oxford · Wien

Christian Thum

Enabling Lightweight Real-time Collaboration

PETER LANG
Internationaler Verlag der Wissenschaften

Bibliographic Information published by the Deutsche Nationalbibliothek
The Deutsche Nationalbibliothek lists this publication in the Deutsche Nationalbibliografie; detailed bibliographic data is available in the internet at http://dnb.d-nb.de.

Zugl.: Mannheim, Univ., Diss., 2011

D 180
ISSN 1616-086X
ISBN 978-3-631-63842-2

www.peterlang.de

Preface

This PhD thesis concludes the research I have conducted during my work as an assistant at the Chair in Information Systems III at the University of Mannheim. Along the course of my doctoral journey I have been supported and inspired by many people.

Above all, I am grateful for the guidance of Prof. Dr. Schader. He did not only encourage me but also gave me the necessary freedom to pursue my research interests. Additionally, I am thankful to Prof. Dr. Heinzl for reviewing my work and giving me valuable advice. Special thanks go to the members of my thesis committee, Prof. Dr. Bauer and Prof. Dr. Engelmann.

Moreover, I am grateful to my colleagues and friends that have contributed much to the success of my dissertation project over the past three years. They have made my PhD a valuable and pleasant experience. In particular, I would like to thank Dr. Stefan Seedorf, Michael Schwind, and Thimo Schulze for reviewing my thesis. I have benefitted much from their feedback. Lastly, and most importantly, I wish to thank my family and my girlfriend, Jenny, for their strong support and encouragement.

Contents

List of Figures

List of Tables

List of Abbreviations

AJAX	Asynchronous JavaScript and XML
API	Application Programming Interface
B2B	Business to Business
B2C	Business to Consumer
CA	Certificate Authority
CATI	Computer-aided Telephone Interview
CAWI	Computer-aided Web Interview
CPU	Central Processing Unit
CSCW	Computer-supported Cooperative Work
CSR	Certificate Signing Request
CSS	Cascading Style Sheets
CWB	Collaborative Web Browsing
DLL	Dynamic Link Library
DNS	Domain Name System
DOM	Document Object Model
HTML	Hypertext Markup Language
HTTP	Hypertext Transfer Protocol
ICT	Information and Communication Technology
IETF	Internet Engineering Task Force
IS	Information Systems
IT	Information Technology

Java EE	Java Enterprise Edition
JDK	Java Development Kit
JRE	Java Runtime Environment
JSF	Java Server Faces
JSON	JavaScript Object Notation
JSP	Java Server Pages
JSR	Java Specification Request
JVM	Java Virtual Machine
kbit/s	kilobit per second
ms	Milliseconds
NIO	Non-blocking Input/Output
OMG	Object Management Group
RAM	Random Access Memory
RCB	Real-time Collaborative Browsing
RFC	Requests for Comments
RIA	Rich Internet Application
RMI	Remote Method Invocation
SaaS	Software as a Service
SDG	Single Display Groupware
SERVQUAL	Service Quality Framework
SLiM	Synchronous Lightweight Modeling
SME	Small and Medium Enterprises
SOP	Same-origin Policy
SSL	Secure Sockets Layer

TCP	Transmission Control Protocol
TTFB	Time To First Byte
UI	User Interface
UML	Unified Modeling Language
URI	Unified Resource Identifier
URL	Unified Resource Locator
VM	Virtual Machine
W3C	World Wide Web Consortium
WHATWG	Web Hypertext Application Technology Working Group
WWW	World Wide Web
XHTML	Extensible Hypertext Markup Language
XML	Extensible Markup Language

1 Introduction

In the age of digitalization, organizations are globally distributed and need to interact across diverse system landscapes with both their partners and customers. Dealing with complex processes requires multiple distributed actors to work on tasks concurrently and to combine their expertise. To this end, they require effective information systems that are collaborative and available on-demand. Ad hoc collaboration and pervasive communication are crucial factors that impact the future competitiveness of organizations (Bughin and Manyika 2007).

In this context, the ubiquity of the Internet creates a host of opportunities and challenges for companies. It has evolved from a read-only information repository to a central application platform that facilitates distributed collaborative work. As such it offers the opportunity to leverage collective knowledge and problem-solving capabilities of geographically dispersed actors by integrating them in a shared environment. Employing traditional collaboration approaches to achieve this goal can be time-consuming and costly (e.g., F. Wang, Rabsch, and Liu 2008). As a consequence, these approaches are not suitable in scenarios where establishing a shared view is solely required for solving one particular task or issues need to be resolved fast. The specific characteristics of so-called ad hoc collaboration scenarios and their associated challenges call for novel, more flexible techniques and tools (e.g., Sengupta, Chandra, and Sinha 2006; Döbler 2007; Whitehead 2007).

1.1 Problem Outline

The first generation of web-based collaboration tools, such as wikis and discussion boards, mainly addressed asynchronous communication requirements. As flexible ways of bringing individuals together in a shared environment they have been adopted in software development projects, for instance (East, Kirby, and Perez 2004; Dekel 2006; Geisser et al. 2007). These tools are easily accessible; hence they have quickly become integral parts of teamwork characterized by dynamic relations between all parties involved. Additionally, many organizations have built Web portals to strengthen collaboration with stakeholders allowing content delivery, content generation, and the integration of enterprise information systems.

Whereas these browser-based solutions have been found to be well-suited to support asynchronous collaboration, real-time collaboration has been difficult to achieve on the Web for a long time (e.g., Esenther 2002a; Atterer, A. Schmidt, and Wnuk 2007, p. 74).

Real-time Web collaboration is a critical complement to asynchronous collaboration. Leveraging collective skills and expertise often does not only require having access to the same information, but rather accessing the same information at the same time. Sharing the same view reduces ambiguities and thereby helps to achieve a common understanding. To provide the benefits of face-to-face meetings in ad hoc online interactions, distributed actors need tools that enable shared visual context. Real-time synchronization of user input can serve to increase productivity by improving communication and knowledge transfer between individuals. Sengupta et al. (2006) underpin this argument with empirical evidence and demand web-based tools that support distributed synchronous activities. The ability to simultaneously discuss and interact with shared objects makes remote collaboration appear more like a face-to-face interaction. In line with this, Karsenty (1999) stresses the importance of shared visual context as a condition to successful interaction in remote collaboration scenarios.

In most cases, synchronous collaboration in heterogeneous environments requires all participants to meet certain technical prerequisites. These include the installation, configuration, and maintenance of the same software on all client systems. As a consequence, real-time collaboration has mainly been restricted to organizations that agree to establish a common collaboration infrastructure. Deployment of such infrastructures is time-consuming and costly. This is inadequate and economically not viable in many situations, especially those where actors need to connect quickly. Moreover, actors might not have the resources, be unwilling, or lack skills to fulfill the prerequisites mentioned. These are some reasons, why novel tools are required to better serve the demands of ad hoc collaboration scenarios. A lightweight collaboration layer, which is non-intrusive and accessible with minimal system requirements regardless of location, is highly desirable.

1.2 Research Questions and Objectives

Given the aforementioned problem statement, the fundamental research objective lies in creating new approaches that facilitate ad hoc collaboration between participants located in heterogeneous environments. Overcoming technical entry barriers arising from diverse system landscapes is an important aspect, because these kinds of settings are becoming increasingly prevalent in today's distributed business processes.

Further investigation is needed to explicate the underlying causes for the barriers to ad hoc collaboration. It stands to reason that the hurdles to collaboration can be lowered by solely building on latest Web technologies and the ubiquitous Web browser as a platform. This has been explored insufficiently in existing literature and therefore should be analyzed in more detail.

In particular, the thesis explores research questions concerning the use of the Web as an enabling technology for synchronous collaboration, including:

- What are the shortcomings of existing collaboration tools with regard to enabling ad hoc collaboration in heterogeneous environments?
- Is it technically feasible to provide a synchronous collaboration layer on top of existing Web content by using only browser-native Web technologies that are available to any Web user?
- Does this collaboration layer facilitate ad hoc collaboration in use cases involving distributed actors in heterogeneous environments? More specifically, can helpdesk services of web-based information systems be improved by employing this type of collaboration layer as a means of live support?

In line with the research questions, the main objective of this thesis is the creation of an innovative IT artifact that allows synchronous web-based collaboration with minimal setup effort. More precisely, the objective is to design and implement a prototype that offers a lightweight, flexible, and secure way of real-time online collaboration. In contrast to current approaches, Web access and the use of a modern browser should be the only requirements users need to fulfill. Further design goals will be derived from specific characteristics of ad hoc collaboration scenarios. To verify the utility of the prototype it is examined how it affects and potentially improves helpdesk and support processes in real-world scenarios.

1.3 Research Methodology

This thesis follows the design science approach (Hevner et al. 2004; 2010) and incorporates the recommendations of Shaw (2002; 2003) for writing "*good software engineering research papers*". The main objective of design-oriented research is to extend organizational capabilities by creating new IT artifacts. These artifacts include methods, models, and software prototypes. Frank (2006) describes the creation and exploration of "*new worlds,*" rather than the study of existing phenomena, as a central feature of research in Information Systems. In this context, Hevner argues in an interview with Winter (2008) that types of rigor applied in other paradigms should not be used in design research in an improvident way. He contends that "*creative inspiration or gut instinct may lead to design decisions*" that cannot be derived from existing theory. Furthermore, he states that when designing an IT artifact it may not be appropriate to base all decisions on grounded behavioral or mathematical theories. In fact, he suggests a reciprocal cause-effect relationship:

> "[...] *theories may as yet be undiscovered or incomplete and the research activities of design and evaluation of the artifact may advance the development and study of such theories.*"
> (Winter 2008, p. 127)

The relevancy gap of Information Systems (IS) as a research discipline is an issue that has been widely debated (Daft and Lewin 1990; Romme 2003). Hevner (2010, p. 13) suggests that although research methods applied in natural sciences are suitable for the study of existing and emerging phenomena, they are often insufficient for solving organizational problems. He states that these problems rather require "*creative, novel and innovative solutions.*" Sometimes design decisions cannot be justified with existing theory, but "*should be evaluated in the light of their practical implications.*" Fettke et al. (2010) present a similar view and conclude that design science research must provide utility for the solution of practical issues.

To this end, the thesis aims to construct an innovative artifact, which improves real-time lightweight collaboration in ad hoc scenarios and is also relevant to practitioners. For this purpose, the software prototype to be designed and implemented was continuously improved and validated in cooperation with industry partners. The prototype was field tested in productive operation. The regular feedback given by industry partners and the experiences gained from performing iterative design cycles ensured that the intended practical value was gained. The requirements and design goals for the artifact construction are systematically derived based on a state-of-the-art review and the business needs identified from the typical use cases. Moreover, a case study is conducted as a means of requirements elicitation and problem analysis. The rationale behind design decisions is presented and discussed in context of the existing knowledge base in the field. During the artifact construction phase, it is noted what contributions the use of particular techniques involve in terms of the intended design goals. In addition to mere software engineering, the verification and experimental evaluation of the innovative IT artifact is of crucial importance. This process is reflected in the outline of this thesis and presented in more detail in the following section.

1.4 Thesis Outline

The thesis comprises six chapters. Its organization and structure is illustrated in Figure 1-1. In chapter 1 the rationale behind the research has been presented along with the problem outline and the research objectives. It has provided a brief overview of the overall methodology for this thesis. More detailed methodological foundations are presented in each chapter when appropriate.

Chapter 2 provides an overview of the underlying theoretical foundations from the realm of computer-supported cooperative work (CSCW) and introduces the problem domain of Web collaboration. Relevant concepts and technologies are outlined. It introduces use cases for live, on-demand collaboration. The extensive problem analysis required by the design science approach is achieved by means of a structured literature review supplemented by an analysis of state-of-the-art approaches to support real-time collaboration on the Web.

Chapter 3 deals with the solution design. It opens by supplementing the problem analysis with a case study which is conducted in a real-world practical setting to ensure that besides well-established domain knowledge actual business needs are also considered. This allows for a more precise determination of relevant requirements and a better identification of perceived deficiencies of existing approaches. The knowledge gained is used to define basic design goals. These serve as guidelines for the construction of an improved solution that advances the state of the art in real-time collaboration.

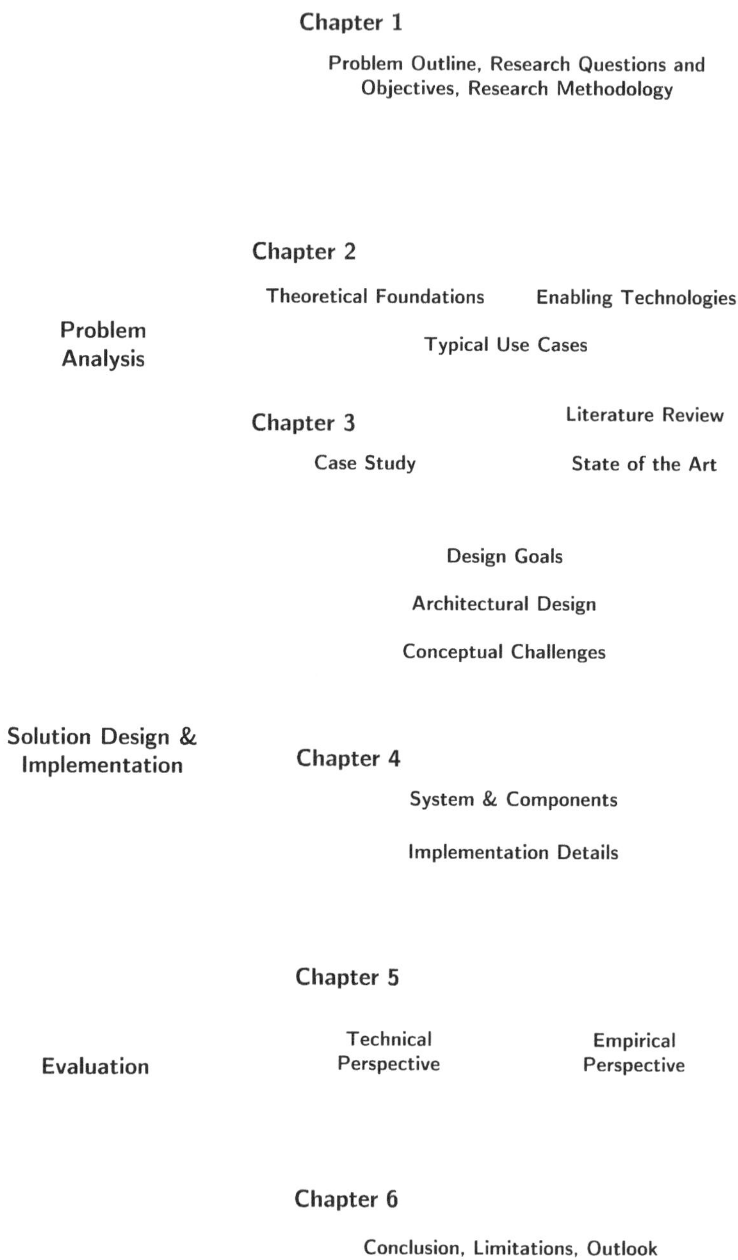

Figure 1-1: Thesis Outline

The remainder of the chapter presents the artifact construction, focusing on the fundamental design decisions concerning the system architecture. Selected conceptual challenges and implications of applying Web 2.0 technologies to real-time collaboration are highlighted. Additionally, possible security issues are taken into consideration. Finally, the problem-solving real-time collaboration system, named synchronite (a portmanteau of the words synchronize and unite), is proposed. This new artifact can be used as a collaboration layer on top of existing single-user Web applications at run-time without altering the original applications.

Chapter 4 deals with the implementation of the artifact as a lightweight, application-agnostic service supporting synchronous work. After providing an overview of the system, the choice of components on the client and server side is explained. Special attention is paid to describe solution approaches which help to overcome problems that previously prevented the implementation of a web-based real-time collaboration system. In this context, an emphasis is put on the description of newly developed proxy techniques, an event synchronization strategy, and multi-user awareness features.

Chapter 5 evaluates the novel artifact from a technical and an empirical perspective. Several experiments are conducted and different components of synchronite are benchmarked against current state-of-the-art solutions. Finally, the constructed prototype is integrated into a campus information system and tested in a real-world scenario comprising heterogeneous clients. The description of the test setup and evaluation is the subject of chapter 5.

Chapter 6 concludes the thesis. The limitations of the constructed solution are presented and an outlook on future research in the domain of Web collaboration is given.

2 Foundations of Web Collaboration

This chapter presents the essentials for the design part of the thesis. To corroborate the practical research objectives from a design science perspective, a concise review of applicable theories is required. As Hevner states in an interview with Winter (2008),

> "*Consideration of rigor in design research is based on the researcher's skilled selection and application of appropriate theories and methods for constructing and evaluating the artifact.*"

Keeping this in mind, the following sections introduce existing theories drawn from the knowledge base of computer-supported cooperative work (CSCW). The relevancy of the design activity is drawn against the background of recent globalization trends, actual business needs, and practices of international collaboration. The chapter lays the foundation for understanding concepts and tools for collaborative work.

2.1 Theoretical Foundations

Selected aspects from the domain of CSCW are discussed in this section. Special features of web-based collaboration are presented against this background. Concomitantly, an introduction of basic concepts and references to the research objectives are made.

2.1.1 Computer-supported Cooperative Work

Along with collaboration across organizational boundaries—reinforced by globalization and Internet availability—distributed work has gained increasing traction in the past years. The idea of using information technology to support collaborative work, however, is not new. In the context of Information Systems, a research discipline dealing with the provision of processes, tools, and technologies for supporting computer-mediated collaboration emerged in the 1980s.

The domain of CSCW encompasses four core areas of research: the creation of new and more efficient approaches, techniques for group-oriented processes, the development of an interdisciplinary understanding of group work (informatics, psychology, sociology, and organization theory), the design and implementation of novel tools for supporting computer-mediated group work, and finally the evaluation of such tools in practical contexts. CSCW has mainly been concerned with groupware applications supporting collaborative text editing and, less frequently, collaborative graphic editing. Modern Web collaboration systems are built upon the basic principles and findings of CSCW. Because of its great popularity, web-based collaboration has emerged as an identifiable research area that focuses on the Web as an infrastructure for collaborative activity.

2.1.2 Dimensions of Collaboration

Although existing literature lacks a widely accepted definition, collaboration is generally described as collective actions of multiple participants toward achieving a mutual goal. In the context of CSCW, collaboration is composed of three layered elements: communication, coordination, and cooperation (Teufel et al. 1995, p. 12).

Communication describes the exchange of information between communication partners and serves as the basis for coordination processes. Coordination is a process embracing all activities required for the reconciliation of shared tasks in the context of teamwork. Realizing coordination in computer-mediated interaction requires both explicit and implicit communication processes. Both ensure that all actors work together in a concerted way to achieve shared goals. Cooperation embodies the rules and structures determining the relationship between participants. It characterizes the degree of "*shared norms and mutually beneficial interactions*" (Thomson and Perry 2006). Complex, interconnected actions require supporting collaboration systems, which mediate the joint and often parallel actions of the participants.

2.1.3 Classification of Collaboration Systems

Several classification methods have been developed in order to delineate different collaboration systems. An early approach was developed by Johansen (1988). He suggests a categorization according to the time and place of collaborative activity. If collaborators work at the same time, collaboration is said to be synchronous. Asynchronous collaboration is the form of joint work where collaborators work at different points in time. As opposed to synchronous activity, collaborators do not see each other's actions in real-time.

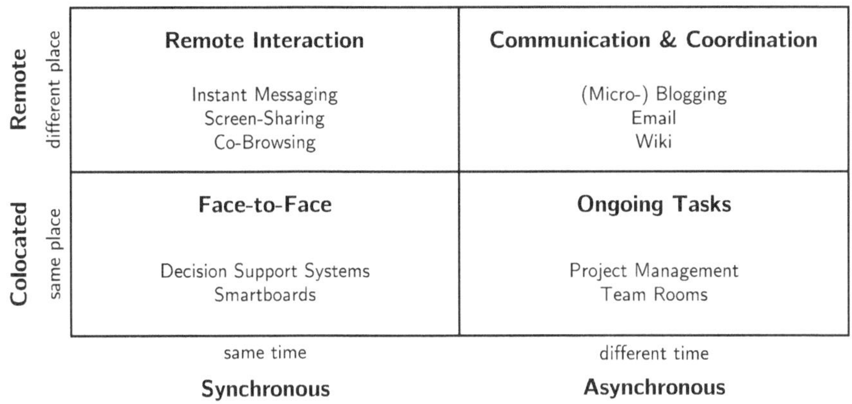

Figure 2-1: CSCW Matrix; adapted from Johansen (1988)

To visualize this concept, Johansen introduced the often quoted "*Any-Time-Any-Place-Matrix*" depicted in Figure 2-1. The prototype presented in this thesis is placed in the highlighted Remote Interaction cell, indicating synchronous collaboration at a distance. Since its first mention, the matrix has been gradually refined and extended. As a third classification factor, Curtis et al. (1988) have introduced an additional organizational dimension which distinguishes inter- or intra-teamwork. French and Layzell (1998) further refine organizational distribution as being inter- or intra-organizational.

In addition to the basic perspective of distribution in time, place, and organization, further dimensions have been presented. For the categorization of lightweight collaboration software most notably the frequency (high, low) and the duration of collaboration engagement (short-term, medium-term, long-term) are crucial. Further criteria for classification of collaboration is elaborated by Theling and Loos (2004), but will not be considered, because it is not deemed relevant for this thesis.

2.2 Enabling Technologies

Jacobson, Booch, and Rumbaugh (2003, p. 28) state that "*tools impact process.*" Keeping this in mind, the conclusion "*technologies impact tools*" seems reasonable. This becomes evident particularly in the domain of computer-supported cooperative work.

Browser-based applications have long been characterized by a lack of user interactivity. Highly interactive tools supporting synchronous collaboration were not considered suitable for the Web and were implemented as desktop applications instead (Whitehead 2007). To create innovative tools, which in turn influence existing processes, new technologies or a purposeful combination of existing technologies are needed. Markus et al. argue that as technologies advance, new kinds of systems and methods are created (Markus, Majchrzak, and Gasser 2002). In this context, the possibilities of the Web (Bentley, Horstmann, and Trevor 1997) and especially the possibilities of the Web 2.0 (Hill et al. 2006) are often referred to as "*enabling technology*". A recent McKinsey study strengthens this argument with empirical evidence:

> "[...] *companies are not only using more* [Web 2.0] *technologies, but also leveraging them to change management practices and organizational structures.*"

2.2.1 The World Wide Web

The Web has fueled a paradigm shift from monolithic software to service-oriented architectures. Ad hoc collaboration and intense interaction are key requirements for the future viability of small and medium-sized enterprises. The demand for interpersonal communication and collaboration is rising. Knowledge workers and organizations are relying on the Web as an infrastructure for collaboration more than ever before (Young et al. 2008; Bughin and Manyika 2007). The Web pervades all processes within and between all stakeholders in today's enterprise ecosystems. It has sustainably accelerated both interaction and information. The browser has transitioned to a ubiquitous runtime environment for applications that can be deployed on-demand.

At the beginning of the millennium, the Web has evolved from an information channel to an interactive application medium. The Web, intended as a read-only information repository, has transitioned into a central platform facilitating distributed collaborative work and knowledge exchange. Although there is no precise definition, the term Web 2.0 is often considered as the technical basis for an increasing number of novel Web applications, so-called Rich Internet Applications (RIA). The term was coined in 2003 by Dale Dougherty and Tim O'Reilly who were seeking to describe new techniques and trends of the Web for a developer conference (O'Reilly 2005).

With emerging Web technologies, an increasing number of desktop-based tools are ported to the Web, which due to their complexity were previously not believed amenable to the browser platform. Traditional desktop applications have turned out to be inadequate for supporting loosely coupled and flexible organizations in today's and future web-based system landscapes: Desktop applications cannot be provisioned at an instant to all participants in a shared environment. Additionally, these tools are usually created as single-user applications restricting flexible access by distributed collaborators—particularly during synchronous activities.

2.2.2 Rich Internet Applications

As outlined above, collaboration on the Web has evolved at a rapid pace. At the same time, the technical requirements on the browser environment have increased. Consequently, in the development of the Web several technologies have aimed at augmenting the capabilities of the Web browser, which was initially designed as a tool for information retrieval only. Developers have tried to overcome the browser barriers and create Rich Internet Applications which offer the responsiveness and capabilities of traditional desktop software. The most commonly used approaches are introduced in the following paragraphs.

Java Applets. Java applets were the first type of technology to bring RIAs to prominence. They allow Java programs to be embedded in a webpage, dynamically loaded over the network, and run locally. Applets abstract from browser differences by relying on the API of the Java Virtual Machine (JVM). Despite the advantages of enabling greater client-side functionality, several drawbacks have negatively impacted the popularity of Java applets:

Java applets—although deployed via the Web browser—run in a separate process. The initial JDK security model ensured that all code downloaded via the network is regarded untrusted and hence run in a restricted and secure environment, referred to as the sandbox. The control policies of the sandbox prevent access to sensitive resources, such as the file system. JDK 1.1 included the capability to digitally sign and verify the Java applets. Code that bears the signature of a trusted entity has full system access and may run operations outside the sandbox. Unsigned or untrusted code is still restricted (Flanagan 2005, p. 303).

It is important to note that this security mechanism is flawed due to the fact that anyone can sign a Java applet. Malicious applets can be signed by an attacker and are then correctly verified and executed by the browser. Thus, browsers require users to confirm a security warning as an additional security measure before permitting the execution of Java applets.

Because malicious Java applets pose a security risk and inexperienced users may allow the execution of potentially harmful applets, many companies have entirely disabled Java functionality within the browser (Zammetti 2008, p. 29).With the advent of Java applets, not all browsers were prepared for their execution. Some were not Java-enabled, while others struggled with inconsistent Java execution environments (e.g., Microsoft J++, Sun JVM). The portability and reusability of Java applets was compromised. Client-side startup is slow as large Java applets require long download times. This was a big concern when Internet connections did not exceed 56 kbit/s downstream and is still noticeable today, although certainly far less than in the past.

Although most of the aforementioned problems are no issue today, Java applets have failed to gain mass adoption (Giguère 2000, p. 36; Zammetti 2006). In fact, today Java is seldom used as a client-side Web programming language, but rather as a server programming language. Some frameworks, such as the Google Web Toolkit[1] allow programmers to code in Java and then translate and compile JavaScript code to be executed in the browser environment.

Browser Plug-ins. Browser plug-ins are extensions that run outside the browser's secure sandbox using low-level browser interfaces to enhance its capabilities by adding functionality. Plug-ins need to be downloaded and installed before use. For security reasons, many users have been reluctant to install browser extensions. This is particularly true for so-called ActiveX components, which are only supported by Microsoft Internet Explorer. Providing a unified and reliable API on all browsers is the greatest advantage of plug-ins. One of the most popular and widely trusted browser plug-ins is Adobe Flash. However, since an increasing number of users browse on mobile devices with different architectures, the importance of native web technologies increases.

1 `http://code.google.com/webtoolkit/`

Browser-native Technologies. Browser-native technologies are included in all major Web browsers and provide a rich experience to users. These technologies encompass JavaScript, DOM (Document Object Model), JSON (JavaScript Object Notation), and XML—a suite of technologies usually referred to as AJAX (Asynchronous JavaScript and XML).

Using asynchronous communication, parts of a webpage can be refreshed separately, without interrupting user activity. This allows higher interactivity and fuels the evolution of the Web from an information medium to a collaboration medium. These new opportunities have elevated the Web to become a platform for the development of innovative tools. In contrast to the browser extension mechanisms described above, AJAX only relies on functionality natively supported by modern Web browsers. As a consequence, browser native technologies like the new HTML 5 standard can also target closed ecosystems (such as iOS) that do not allow external plug-ins such as Adobe Flash.

2.2.3 Web Browsers as Universal Runtime Environments

Whilst the Web was characterized by one way communication and information retrieval, Rich Internet Applications have enabled social interaction and cooperative teamwork. Of the various browser extension mechanisms discussed, only Adobe Flash has gained widespread distribution. Java applets are still used in certain cases where the advantage of increased client functionality outweighs the disadvantages described above. To conclude, new Web technologies should work inside the browser, i.e., be native to the browser without requiring the installation of extensions unfamiliar to users.

In a short period of time, Web browsers have evolved to ubiquitous runtime environments and many desktop-based applications are ported to the Web. In fact, many webpages should more accurately be labeled Web applications due to their heavy use of AJAX. Leveraging the Web as a channel for software delivery is gaining importance and increasing acceptance. It frees end-users and IT departments from the administrative burden of software configuration and maintenance. In addition, the Web channel allows universal access independent of location and workstation.

2.3 Typical Use Cases

Web collaboration encompasses many different scenarios. In general, the choice of adequate tool support depends on the specifics of the use case such as the distribution of actors, their relationship, and the ways they interact (Dennis, Fuller, and Valacich 2008; Niinimäki et al. 2010). Therefore, it is essential to investigate the scenarios targeted by the novel collaboration service in more detail and explicate their specific characteristics.

2.3.1 Characteristics

As sketched in the problem outline, to this point all client systems must typically meet technical requirements to participate in a collaboration session. Necessary preparations include the download, installation, and configuration of third-party software. Hence, the use of collaboration software has been merely intra-organizational or limited to scenarios where a common IT infrastructure exists.

Nevertheless, there is a continuous and growing demand for a real-time collaboration environment, most notably in scenarios for which various reasons prevent the establishment of a common infrastructure. In these cases, the only common denominator is usually a Web browser. Lightweight real-time collaboration targets situations where the use of any additional software to accommodate collaboration is not a valid option. These situations include those in which

- actors need to initiate collaboration in an instant and lack the time or resources to fulfill the prerequisites;
- setting up a common IT infrastructure is economically not viable;
- limited privileges in corporate domains may impose an additional barrier, making traditional collaboration tools impossible to use;
- users may be inexperienced or computer-illiterate and thus unable to install, download, and configure software; or
- cautious users may be reluctant to take risks by installing third-party software or confirming security dialogs that request the execution of collaborative browser extensions.

Based on the classification framework introduced in section 2.1.3, the targeted use cases can be categorized as being synchronous, remote, and characterized by low-frequency and short-term engagement. In other words, an emphasis is put on supporting short-term collaboration in situations where collective activity is occasional or spontaneous. The need for collaboration does not arise regularly, but when required, collaboration support has to be available in an instant without requiring any effort. In this context, the benefit of a lightweight real-time collaboration system that only relies on browser-native functionality becomes evident. Some of these scenarios are sketched in more detail below.

2.3.2 Guided Live Support

Given the rapid development in the field of web-based information systems, an increasing number of products and services are delivered online. Web-based applications targeted at end users are becoming increasingly complex and knowledge-intensive. Multiple studies provide evidence that users have trouble completing common tasks online. Consequently, it has become increasingly important for organizations to provide support services and assist their customers. Applications from the domains of e-government, finance, and healthcare, for example, provide customer self-service for complex tasks that many users are not familiar with. At the same time, some of these tasks are of vital importance; therefore, it must be ensured that the system is used correctly. This drives the demand for web-based collaboration. Interactive live support by collaborative browsing can help to train, educate, and guide users of such systems. Van Velsen et al. (2007) argue that the strategic importance of adequate user support is being recognized by more and more companies. In the context of online support, the promotional role of ad hoc collaboration may be further emphasized. Service staff can engage in a personal dialog with their customers. With live support, customers can get immediate assistance from technical advisors who can navigate the site with them, resolve issues and point them in the right direction. This encounter impacts the image of the organization as well as its products and services. In these kinds of scenarios, providing a lightweight collaborative environment can be regarded as a measure of increasing customer retention. As live support processes are of particular importance in the realm of e-commerce, the following description is based on this domain.

2.3.3 Guided Sales

As a consequence of the increasing number of goods and services delivered via web shops, the demand for online support rises. According to a recent study conducted by tns infratest in 2010, 71 percent of customers in the B2C distance selling segment in Germany are leveraging the Internet rather than traditional ways of ordering, such as the telephone or postal mail (BVH 2010, p. 5).

While the number of online shoppers continues to grow, studies show that many are unable to find the desired information or get stuck in the complicated navigational issues. Besides other important drivers, being unable to resolve issues in a personal dialog with a customer service representative might lead to the often quoted "*cart abandonment phenomenon*", an issue frustrating many online retailers. Despite putting items in virtual shopping carts, customers often quit the shopping process without completing the purchase. Industry studies show evidence that 88 percent of online shoppers have abandoned their shopping cart (Johnson, Wilson, and Meyer 2005). Andersen Consulting and Forrester Research report cart abandonment rates of 25% (Kukar-Kinney and Close 2009). According to Jupiter Research (2008), only 64% of filled shopping carts eventually result in a purchase. Although customers want to gather information and make their own decisions, they actively seek help and support of advisors. In an attempt to satisfy these demands live chats have been deployed. This is evidence of a growing industry awareness of the customers' demand for help and guidance. Contrary to traditional telephone helplines, live chats allow users to avoid media breaks, hence limiting the inhibition to contact service staff. While the need to communicate via the telephone is eliminated, a common view that could help increase the quality of the interaction is still missing. Frambach et al. (2007, p. 36) identify the ability to contact a sales advisor as a major driver determining the online or offline channel preference. It strongly impacts the consumers' decision to buy.

Sharing the same view can bridge a gap between online and offline shops: Ad hoc collaboration establishes instant connections between customers and sales/service staff allowing agents or service representatives to view customers' browsers in real-time. Agents can assist customers in online shops by explaining complex services or product configurations. This is particularly useful in scenarios where products and services are characterized by low conversion rates, but high-value transactions.

In the first generation e-commerce, the items sold online were mostly simple to understand products like books, software, and music. Nowadays, even complex products which are inherently challenging to sell are marketed online. Examples include products like cell phones contracts, mortgages and investment assets. Only a few empirical studies have investigated the characteristics of the decision-making process when acquiring complex products on the Internet. According to Vroomen et al. (2005), complex products and services are typically "*tailor-made, infrequently purchased, more difficult to comprehend, and require in general assistance during the decision-making process*". Coughlan et al. (2011, p. 150) argue that complex services, such as insurance policies are even more difficult to understand when transferred to the e-commerce market because of the "*reduction of human assistance*" in the consumption process.

In this respect, collaborative browsing can contribute to closing the gap between the offline and online market place. Advisor-client interactions can effectively supplement and add value to many services delivered via the online channel. Assisted browsing may uncover a potential for personalized up- and cross-selling similar to that in offline shops. This can ease the order process, making communication with sales staff more vivid, efficient, and enhance the customer's experience. Making the customer feel more involved and informed can help allay his or her confusion and support the decision process. In this context, Forrester Research has recently stressed the importance of the Web to connect advisors and clients (Doyle et al. 2011). The research group particularly emphasizes the importance in the financial sector, where most conversations between clients and advisors happen remotely—usually over the phone. They argue that assisted browsing can supplement the audio connection by providing visual support, which enables clients to view and discuss their portfolio online at any time. Forrester Research states that more than 25 percent of affluent US investors express interest in online collaborative advice tools.

2.3.4 Guided Surveys

When prospective customers are asked to give their opinion of product designs and characteristics; it is important that the process of retrieving the opinion is efficient and produces as little effort as possible for the participant. Consequently, data is often collected via inexpensive online surveys also called computer-aided Web interviews (CAWI) or using computer-aided telephone interviews (CATI) rather than face-to-face interviews. While CAWI and CATI surveys are low cost and allow for a high level of standardization, they are not without limitations (Pfeffermann and Rao 2009, p. 191). They are bound to gather simple data requiring short and easy to understand questions. Due to the lack of shared visual context, respondents may not be able to concentrate on the survey. In CATI surveys there is no way of visualizing complex issues. In CAWI surveys respondents cannot ask questions for clarification of ambiguous survey items. As a result, any qualitative information retrieved may be of poor quality.

Using a lightweight real-time collaboration service, call agents can visualize complex interviews (such as conjoint analyses) on the screens of respondents. No installation or download is required and all security policies may remain activated. This enables the call agent to clarify problems, guide the respondent, and explain complex questions with visual support. Respondents can verify that the call agent records the answers correctly. The synchronization of browser contents may help increase the validity of measurement by decreasing the response bias.

2.3.5 Collaborative Software Development

Cooperation across organizational boundaries in software development projects is becoming ever more important due to a number of reasons. Distributed development teams face several challenges, some of which can be tackled by employing collaboration software. At first, collaborative platforms mainly addressed asynchronous communication requirements of distributed development teams by providing facilities such as wiki and forums. While teams can benefit from these tools, often more sophisticated tools are needed to support collaboration in highly synchronous scenarios, such as the modeling and design phase. Being able to initiate ad hoc meetings and to work on tasks concurrently enables each team member to leverage collective skills and expertise. Therefore, development teams need adequate support from real-time collaboration software that helps increasing productivity by improving communication and knowledge transfer between individuals.

With emerging Web technologies novel tools have been created permitting the flexible integration of distributed collaborators during development activities, which due to their complexity were not believed amenable to lightweight collaboration tools. The need for real-time collaboration has for instance been addressed by presenting SLiM, a lightweight environment for synchronous modeling that runs in unmodified browsers and enables dispersed development teams to collaborate on UML diagrams (Thum, Schwind, and Schader 2009). The emphasis was on dynamic environments where ad hoc practices are applied, e.g., globally distributed open source initiatives. The SLiM prototype has been continuously enhanced and is subject to ongoing development in the research project GlobaliSE[2] which started in April 2009 and is funded by the Ministry of Science, Research and Arts of the federal state Baden-Württemberg. The project's main objective is to create advanced methods and tools that enable SMEs to use their specific strengths in the face of great economic pressure.

2.3.6 Social Shopping

Although social commerce is gaining importance in the context of the recent success of large-scale social networks, online shopping so far remains a solitary experience. As Zhu et al. (2010) state consumers in the e-commerce domain often desire to conduct and share their shopping activities with others. Deploying a real-time collaboration layer in a consumer-to-consumer scenario can allow multiple individuals to interact in online shops. Thereby, the joint shopping experience of real-world shops can be transferred to the online domain. This use case is also described by Wiltse and Nichols (2009) who emphasize the potentially great emotional appeal of joint online shopping. The social online experience may improve buying decisions, enhance the overall shopping process, and thereby increase sales.

2.3.7 Summary

Users in the scenarios sketched above have great potential of gaining benefits from real-time collaboration, but so far have been unable to realize it. There is a need to investigate the underlying reasons. To concentrate the thesis, interactive live support has been chosen as the main area of focus. The requirements derived for this scenario are mostly applicable in the other use cases described.

2 `http://www.globalise-projekt.de`

2.4 State of the Art

Design-oriented research requires a comprehensive review of state-of-the-art approaches. For this purpose, the section follows the basic guidelines of conducting a structured and effective literature review (cf. J. Webster and Watson 2002; Torraco 2005; Okoli and Schabram 2010). In order to adequately address research gaps and provide a firm foundation for the solution design, it is crucial to identify and analyze the already available knowledge. In line with this, Winter (2008) emphasizes that it must be clear what kind of similarities and differences exist compared to existing IT artifacts. It is only after having reviewed past approaches that the technical requirements and design aspects of a real-time collaboration tool can be discussed. Focus is placed, in particular, on the collaborative capabilities provided by today's network meeting tools and the infrastructure and system requirements necessary for their deployment. Minimizing these is a crucial factor impacting the adoption and efficiency of collaboration tools (Kaiser et al. 1998; Campbell 2002a; Campbell 2002b). In the following, the review strategy and criteria used for classification of existing network meeting tools is introduced.

2.4.1 Review Strategy

To build up an initial pool of primary papers the keywords "*real-time Web collaboration*", "*collaborative browsing*", and "*synchronous browsing*" were used on freely available meta search engines such as Google Scholar[3], Scirus[4], and CiteSeerX[5]. The initial search for Web collaboration systems revealed a disproportionate number of conceptual approaches, rather than architecture descriptions or concrete implementations. Due to the strong commercial interest, more specific details are typically not disclosed within the scope of academic papers, but filed as patents. As a consequence the search was continued at a broader scope including patent search engines such as Google Patent Search[6] and FreePatents Online[7]. Once an initial set of primary papers was identified, backward and forward searching techniques as recommended by Levy and Ellis (2006) were applied. In the backward search, the references cited in the

3 http://scholar.google.com

4 http://www.scirus.com

5 http://citeseerx.ist.psu.edu

6 http://patents.google.com

7 http://www.freepatentsonline.com

primary papers found were retrieved and analyzed. In the final forward search follow-up approaches and newer solutions were located by searching for papers that reference or cite relevant primary articles. Complementary to this, future work by the authors of primary articles is checked for relevance to the field under study. All related work identified within the search was systematically analyzed according to the review criteria elaborated in the following section.

In summary, the review does not only take into account academic research prototypes from the domain of computer-supported cooperative work, but also commercial network meeting tools. Combining these perspectives allows gaining insights about existing CSCW research and other relevant domains. This supports deriving requirements for a novel solution that is based on existing knowledge and driven by clear business needs.

2.4.2 Review Criteria

In the context of this thesis, existing tool-centric approaches are reviewed and evaluated with regard to their adequacy for shared Web browsing scenarios as outlined in the previous section (see section 2.3). The criteria chosen aims for a classification of state-of-the-art approaches according to a functional and technological dimension. An emphasis is put on the technological dimension as it is the key to realizing a lightweight solution that reduces entry barriers to collaboration. The characteristics of the two dimensions chosen are described in the next sections.

Functional Dimension. The functional dimension describes the collaborative capabilities offered (i.e., the general adequacy of the tool for synchronous real-time collaboration). Limited functionality is provided by tools that merely allow input control to rest with one designated presenter (one-to-many), which is typical for screen sharing tools. Adequate functionality for the purpose of simultaneous work is provided when all collaborators can synchronously edit a shared object and the changes made are reflected on either side in real-time (many-to-many). In summary, tools are considered suitable for highly synchronous scenarios if they permit interactive multi-user collaboration and provide collaborative browsing features such as collaborative editing of Web forms and collaborative navigation of websites.

Technological Dimension. The platform used for realizing collaboration support determines the placement along the technological dimension. Furthermore, this placement implies the system requirements with which participating clients need to comply. It is an indicator for the ease of setting up the collaboration environment (software installation, configuration, and maintenance effort). A distinction is drawn between internet-based, web-based, browser-based, and browser-native platforms. The individual characteristics of the different types of applications are outlined in the following paragraphs.

Because the terms Internet and Web are often used synonymously, a more precise demarcation is necessary. Many applications are declared being web-based, although they establish independent Internet connections to proprietary servers or clients outside the Web (Dix 1997). Such Internet applications, which do not adhere to the Web standard for communication, the Hyper Text Transfer Protocol (HTTP), or do not use HTTP exclusively, will be categorized as internet-based applications.

The subset of internet-based applications adhering to Web standards is designated as being web-based. Using HTTP as a communication protocol is mandatory, i.e., the use of proprietary protocols is not allowed. Web-based systems do not necessarily rely on the Web browser as an execution environment, but can have separate client programs with user interfaces like standard desktop software. These platform-dependent client programs can limit the portability and impede the deployment to heterogeneous environments.

Solutions that retain the advantage of being interoperable across heterogeneous environments and increase accessibility and availability at the same time use a browser-based (plug-ins allowed) or a browser-native approach (no plug-ins allowed). Alternative terms used for this architecture in research papers are "*web-native solutions*" (M. Webster 2005), "*unmodified browser*" (Keukelaere et al. 2008) and "*browser-based without plug-ins*" (Ono 2008). Table 2-2 summarizes the classification scheme used to categorize collaboration systems by application platform. The categories are contrasted and delineated by the key characteristics outlined above.

Browser-native applications are often described as zero-footprint or lightweight, as no installation or configuration on client systems is required and the applications rely only on functionality natively supported by modern Web browsers. This reduces the system requirements for clients who intend to engage in collaborative activities. Based on the HTTP

		Application Platform			
		internet-based	web-based	browser-based	browser-native
Characteristics	Communication only via HTTP(S)-Protocol		●	●	●
	User Interface resides entirely in the web browser			●	●
	No Extenstions such as plug-ins, Flash, Java, ActiveX				●

Table 2-2: Characteristics of Application Platforms

protocol, it is possible to provide a cost-effective location- and platform-independent solution. Browser-based and browser-native applications offer several advantages compared to traditional desktop applications.

Table 2-1 illustrates the implications for each of the distinct application platforms. The low system requirements—Web access and usage of a modern browser—relieve companies from the administrative burden of setting up and maintaining a dedicated IT infrastructure. There is no need for the installation of separate desktop clients. The larger the number of external participants in collaborative scenarios and the more heterogeneous their system landscapes, the more evident the advantage of a

		Application Platform			
		internet-based	web-based	browser-based	browser-native
Implications	No Configuration of network or firewall		●	●	●
	No Download of third-party access programs			●	●
	No Installation of additional software or browser extensions				●
	No Maintenance such as manual client-side version updates				●
	No Footprint client systems are not modified				●

Table 2-1: Ease of Deployment by Application Platforms

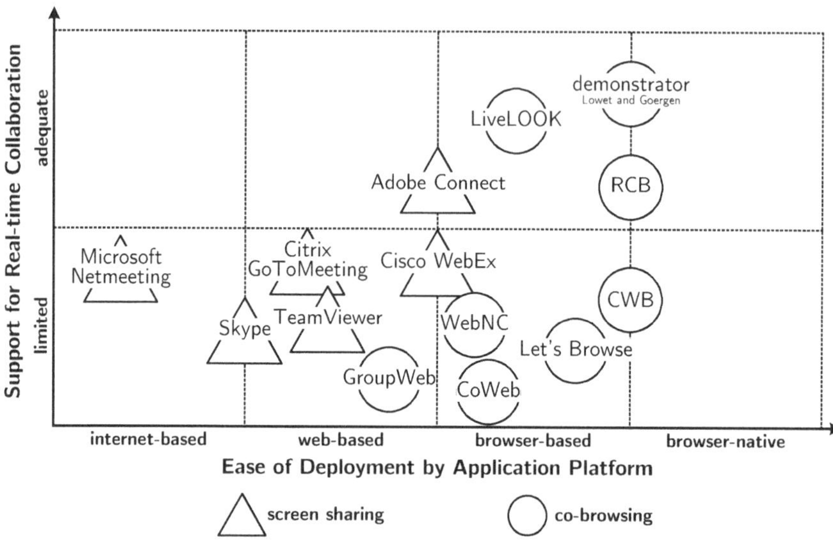

Figure 2-2: Classification of Related Work

browser-based or browser-native solution becomes. Both types of application, browser-based and browser-native, are loaded from the Web server prior to their execution in the Web browser. Therefore, the deployment effort is reduced and advantages can be realized. For instance, applications can be updated and extended by additional functionality without requiring manual client-side software updates. This avoids software version conflicts and inconsistencies among clients. The next section provides an overview of existing collaboration systems to support synchronous access to Web resources.

2.4.3 Classification of Related Work

All considered tools aim to improve communication, interaction, and the collaborative work of remote participants. Also, related tools that originally were not created for these generic purposes, but allow real-time collaboration are considered with regard to the above-mentioned classification criteria and relevant design aspects. The approaches reviewed are placed in the classification matrix depicted in Figure 2-2 according to the functional and technological dimensions outlined in the previous section.

In general, existing work can be categorized as screen sharing, co-browsing, and novel real-time Web collaboration solutions, which are visually highlighted in the matrix. The vertical dimension describes the breadth of collaborative capabilities offered and the degree of support for real-time collaboration. The placement along the horizontal dimension determines the application platform and thereby the ease of deployment. This allows a characterization and discrimination of tools with respect to their adequacy for highly synchronous scenarios. The best fit according to the selected dimensions is achieved in the top right corner. With regard to screen sharing, many tools offer similar features. In purpose of clarity, related tools that provide identical functionality or only have negligible differences are omitted in the figure.

Generic web collaboration tools like WebEx[8] and Adobe Connect[9] allow online meetings and distributed use of any application installed on the client PC. Employing screen sharing tools has to be evaluated critically with regard to the requirement of ad hoc availability in highly dynamic, loosely coupled environments. Special access programs need to be downloaded or installed and may require administrative staff with special privileges. Furthermore, generic tools do not allow for simultaneous work. Typically, only one user can have input control at a time. Simultaneous access to the shared application is not supported; hence, team productivity is limited to a restrictive presenter-viewer role allocation.

Adobe Connect depends on the Adobe Flash plug-in, which has to be installed or updated in order to allow participants to join the meeting. In cases where the plug-in is pre-installed, immediate access to the meeting is possible. The meeting host, however, is additionally required to download and install the Adobe Connect add-in which runs outside the browser and places UI-components in the system tray. Hence, the categorization of Adobe Connect is ambiguous. The participant's side is browser-based whereas the meeting host who requires a third-party plug-in is regarded web-based. A similar constellation applies to the WebEx conferencing solution: The client's viewing capability is browser-based. The meeting host is web-based as download and execution of a separate client program is necessary.

WebNC is a system for sharing and viewing Web applications. It periodically captures the viewport of the browser as an image encoded in tiles and delivers bandwidth adaptive images to clients. The viewing users can begin collaboration immediately as only JavaScript and HTML are re-

8 `http://www.webex.com`

9 `http://www.adobe.com/products/acrobatconnectpro/`

quired. The meeting host (e.g., presenter), however, needs to have the proprietary WebNC browser extension that is only available for Mozilla Firefox (Denoue et al. 2009). Collaboration support is limited as participants can only view the actions performed by the meeting host, but not perform actions themselves.

Conventional screen sharing products record screen contents in the form of a video stream and forward it via high-performance media servers to participating clients. Most existing screen capturing and streaming tools rely on sophisticated encoding techniques. Differences between two subsequent screen shots are identified and only the changed image parts are transmitted to decrease bandwidth usage. This is appropriate for desktop sharing.

For sharing Web content, a more efficient approach is possible that leverages the special nature of browser-based applications: By rendering websites natively inside a Web browser and not as image data, these approaches provide a better user experience and adaption to different screen resolutions. These specialized so-called co-browsing solutions allow multiple participants to collaboratively navigate websites in a synchronized way. Researchers in the field of CSCW have pointed out the need for browser-enabled synchronous work since the late 90s (Graham 1997; Jacobs et al. 1996; Roseman and Greenberg 1996). In fact, so-called co-browsing systems have been continuously researched in the context of CSCW for more than ten years. Several solutions exist that allow co-browsing of websites. First-generation approaches are limited to pushing the same URL to each client browser neglecting the synchronization of events within webpages. This is particularly unfavorable when browsing highly dynamic webpages or using RIAs, which run entirely within the context of a single page. Chong and Sakauchi (2000) argue that

> *"Web browsers have not yet found a satisfactory transition into the realm of multi-user collaborative applications except for very basic Web co-navigation functionality, which only ensures that all browsers display the same URL [...]."*

Another problem of pure URL-pushing approaches identified by Yue et al. (2009) is that the scope of webpages eligible for this method is limited. He states that session protected webpages cannot be accessed by simply copying the URL. Moreover, for many dynamic webpages that make heavy use of AJAX the content may be different even though the same URL is displayed in the browser's address bar.

GroupWeb and GroupScape are special groupware Web browsers implemented for the purpose of allowing users to visually share and navigate static webpages (Roseman and Greenberg 1996; Graham 1997). Chong and Sakauchi (2000) criticize this approach, because the groupware client has to be updated for compatibility as Web standards are developed. Browser-based solutions such as CoWeb (Jacobs et al. 1996) or Let's Browse (Lieberman, Van Dyke, and Vivacqua 1999) require all participants to install browser extensions such as the Java Runtime Environment (JRE) or proprietary plug-ins.

The transition of the Web from an information channel to an interactive medium (see section 2.2.1) gave new momentum to research in the field of real-time Web collaboration. Increasingly interactive, highly dynamic Web applications put new requirements on synchronization mechanisms that are not met by co-browsing solutions designed for static websites. Esenther (2002a) presents Collaborative Web Browsing (CWB), a browser-native lightweight solution for Microsoft's Internet Explorer that does not require any user setup, but is limited to co-browsing websites hosted on the same domain. The system consists of a controller module that runs on the Web server hosting the pages to be co-browsed and a Java Script client that runs on the client-side. The client notifies the controller module about local changes and regularly polls for remotely executed changes.

Lowet and Goergen (2009) present a co-browsing solution that is capable of synchronizing dynamic interactions on webpages. It is implemented as a demonstrator on networked television sets and allows joint form-filling and scrolling. They overcome restrictions imposed by the browser, e.g., the same-origin policy (see section 3.4.1), by asking the user for additional security privileges, such as cross-site scripting and special use of TCP sockets. This is not only a potential security risk, but it also limits the use of the application to specific browsers. In addition, in many ad hoc collaboration scenarios it is highly undesirable to ask users to take risks by allowing critical access to their computers.

Yue et al. (2009) describe a browser-based approach called Real-time Collaborative Browsing (RCB) that is based on two components. The user hosting the collaborative session is required to install a browser plug-in, the so-called RCB-Agent. Joining users must visit a specially prepared webpage that has and embedded JavaScript RCB client. Using the extension mechanism, RCB allows users to jointly view and operate websites. Although an adequate support for real-time collaboration is achieved, the usage of a proprietary browser extension mechanism restricts collaborative browsing to certain client systems. Another limitation is constituted by the fact that webpages need to have the RCB Java Script Client embedded to be prepared for co-browsing. Moreover, the browser plug-in is only available for Microsoft Internet Explorer and Mozilla Firefox.

Industry interest in co-browsing and related technology is high. As a consequence, few descriptions of architecture and implementation details of such systems are disclosed in academic literature. Conversely, multiple related patents have been filed describing various systems and methods to set up transparent proxies and allow collaborative viewing and navigation of webpages. This demonstrates strong practical and commerical relevance. In US-Patent No. 6151622, Fraenkel and Kishan (2000) describe a method approach for serializing and replicating Web documents comprised of multiple frames. In US-Patent No. 2002/0138624A1, Esenther (2002b) presents a system that uses a monitor to regularly poll for changes to a webpage including input in form fields and the currently visible area of the webpage. The serialized state information is then copied to participating client browsers.

2.4.4 Summary

Despite several advances in the field of Web collaboration, most of the developments have been limited to support basic URL-push functionality or collaborative form-filling on static webpages. There is currently no widespread real-time shared-browsing service. Several commercial products as well as academic research prototypes exist, all of which are limited by at least one of the following deficiencies:

- dependence on proprietary protocols;
- dependence on specific browsers;
- no replication and handover of Web sessions;
- no support for synchronization of JavaScript events;
- no support for dynamic AJAX content;
- mandatory installation, download or configuration of browser plugins or extensions.

It is an objective to overcome these perceived deficiencies and thereby advance the state of the art of Web collaboration.

3 Solution Design

This chapter focuses on the elaboration of the design goals. These are derived as functional and non-functional requirements from the specific characteristics of the typical use cases (see section 2.3) and the preceding state-of-the-art review. The design goals outlined are used to guide the construction of the solution design.

After presenting an overview of the architecture of the proposed lightweight approach, it is shown how the particular deficiencies of existing solutions are overcome. The proposed solution design is a generalization of the specific collaboration architecture originally tailored to support the process of synchronous modeling (Thum et al. 2009). Innovative techniques are applied which only rely on functionality natively supported by modern Web browsers. The architecture avoids technical issues that previously impeded clients to be integrated into collaborative environments and facilitates ad hoc collaboration on arbitrary Web applications.

Following the design-oriented approach, the techniques used for the construction of the novel IT artifact are documented comprehensively. This permits third parties to assimilate and gain knowledge about the techniques.

3.1 Case Study

In order to supplement the knowledge derived from the literature review with a practical perspective, this section presents requirements derived from two qualitative case studies. The first study is conducted with support agents working at the helpdesk and the second study with selected experienced users of the service. Data is collected through semi-structured face-to-face interviews.[10] The dialog between the researcher and the respondents is guided by the set of interview questions listed in Appendix 0 and 0. As suggested by Strauss and Corbin (2008, p. 32) the research questions are open and not strictly framed in order to allow the

10 The underlying data was collected in 2010 by Jan Mollner during his time as a student assistant at the Chair in Information System III at the University of Mannheim and is also analyzed in the context of his bachelor thesis.

flexibility to explore the requirements and issues as identified by the respondents. First, the objectives of the interview are stated. Then it is explained that the interview is recorded and transcribed for later analysis.

As some interview questions aim to gather potentially sensitive information, e.g., regarding the respondents' competence, they are assured that only anonymous data would be presented. Respondents are encouraged to comment on their everyday work processes, tools, and the challenges faced. To avoid misunderstandings, the major findings are summarized by the researcher towards the end of the interview (cf. Runeson and Höst 2008, p. 146).

3.1.1 Context of the Study

The University of Mannheim uses a campus information system to provide services to various stakeholders including students and academic staff. In particular, services relating to the teaching process are offered. Students can use the system to register to seminars, check their grades, and browse the lecture catalog. Academic staff can schedule lectures, request rooms, and enter students' grades. The campus information system has about 10,000 registered students, 790 members of academic and 550 members of administrative staff.

In everyday operation situations arise in which portal users encounter problems or require assistance in solving a particular task they cannot complete by themselves. Assistance by trained support agents is available via email or a telephone helpline. In addition, users are provided with online manuals, contact forms, and can register for scheduled training sessions. Agents usually provide step-by-step instructions tailored to solving the specific problem of the requester. The research questions aim to explore how support processes are typically handled and which problems occur with respect to communication.

3.1.2 Support Agents

The first case study was conducted with personnel of the helpdesk services at the data processing center of the University of Mannheim. Data is collected to obtain knowledge about issues with support requests and potential areas for improvement.

The respondents include the project manager responsible for the operation of the campus information system (respondent A) and two experienced support agents working at the helpdesk (respondent B, C). In the following, the major issues identified by the support agents are described. Subsequently, the requirements elicited from the interview are presented.

Concerns and Issues. The interviews underpin the assumption that delivering support via telephone or email is difficult due to a lack of shared visual context (cf. section 2.3.2). Users often struggle to describe to the support agent what they are seeing on their screen. Respondent A describes typical communication efforts when trying to comprehend problem descriptions given by users in a telephone support scenario:

> "*With the current tools [telephone line] in use there is always a delay. Additionally, there are communication problems. What does it mean when you say top left? It takes some time to recognize what [users] mean when they say top left.*"

In turn, support agents find it cumbersome to give step-by-step instructions via the telephone. This problem is exacerbated by the language barrier between IT staff and administrative employees. Respondent C explains the communication issues as a source of confusion between support agents and users: "*I ask users to click on a drop down list. And [some users] do not know what a drop down list or form is.*"

To overcome this problem, various screen sharing tools such as Microsoft NetMeeting, TeamViewer, and Skype (see 2.1.3) have been tested. Respondent C reports on experience with screen sharing solutions and states that it has been unsatisfactory due to technical difficulties: "*I have personally used Windows NetMeeting. But when one user operates Windows 7 and I use [Windows] XP, it does not work.*" This quote confirms the barriers formed by high usage requirements of traditional network meeting tools. Support agents explain that when no screen sharing solution can be used, screenshots are sent via email instead. All respondents identify the need for shared visual context as an important prerequisite to support users appropriately. The requirements towards the solution design are outlined in the next section.

Solution Requirements and Suggestions. Respondent B summarizes that it would be better to see what the user does and check if he understood the instruction given to him on the phone. Respondent A points out:

> *"It would be really great if you could show users where they should move the mouse and highlight that area or do something else to visually mark it for the users. 'This is top left.' At the same time, we must see in real-time if the user has in fact clicked on what he wanted to click."*

The quote above illustrates the need for awareness features and the synchronization of mouse gestures. Respondent C stresses the importance of the support solution to function independently of the platform in use. Regarding the process of initiating collaboration with users the support agents make concrete suggestions:

> *"I imagine the simplest solution as follows: Support-seeking users call us. They are logged on to the Web portal [campus information system] and I can send them a message and then a window pops up [on their screens]. This would be the easiest way to start collaboration. Otherwise, if I send a link via email he might read it in two days or too late."* (Respondent B)

The idea of initiating the collaboration session by simply choosing the users from a list of active portal visitors and sending a support message their browser is also appreciated by the other respondents. They add that the popup window should be clearly visible and overlay the Web portals content. Respondent A requests that the live support solution should allow multiple parallel sessions. Moreover, he suggests that one support agent should be able to request the help of another agent who is an expert regarding one specific topic. This would enable agents to forward sessions to each other and cooperatively answer the user's question.

3.1.3 Lead Users

The second case study was conducted with two lead users who have several years of experience in using the campus management system (respondents A and B). The lead users were chosen by the project manager of the campus information system based on their experience. As recommended by Runeson and Höst (2008, p. 147) care was taken to select respondents who differ with respect to job role and personality. Respondent A is a member of the academic staff whereas respondent B is working as an administrative assistant. Both users regularly use the campus information system in their everyday work processes. They are familiar with basic functionalities of the module catalog and regularly perform tasks such as registering new lectures, allocating rooms, and entering students' exam grades. Additionally respondent A uses the e-learning features of the Web portal. Following von Hippel (1988), interviewing lead users can help to generate ideas that may be overseen when simply examining deficiencies of state-of-the-art solutions. He argues they will help invent solutions that meet their own advanced needs. The study seeks to better understand specific factors that are driving users' attitudes towards the support service and gain insights about respondents. To this end, the objective is to identify problems with the current support process and elicit business needs and requirements. This information is then incorporated into the design of an improved solution. The following section communicates the findings of the study and presents the major issues identified by the lead users.

Concerns and Issues. Both respondents report a major reason for contacting support is that things simply cannot be found. They describe to struggle with frequent changes in the structure of the Web portal:

> "*Another problem that I often have is that the pages in the student portal change fast, i.e., frequently. And then you wonder, I have done this before, but somehow now everything looks very different, and is arranged in a totally different order.*"

Respondent B adds that occasionally problems also arise from insufficient access rights. Tasks such as creating a lecture or editing details afterwards are perceived to be complex. When respondents feel they cannot cope with the task themselves, they mainly seek help by calling the helpdesk personnel. They are aware of the email contact form and the ticket system, but prefer to be helped via phone instead. Respondent B notes that it is not always obvious what number to call when having a specific problem. The promptness of the answer is very important as respondent A explains:

> "*[...] help by email or ticket system takes too long. Because when I have a problem, I want it to be resolved now and as quickly as possible and [I] do not want to invest a lot of time now or later.*"

Although respondents are satisfied with the promptness of the solution offered via telephone, they agree to have trouble both communicating their problem and comprehending the solution steps given by the support agents. Respondent B clarifies:

> "*So I think one issue is often that the user cannot explain what exactly the problem is or he describes the problem in a manner that*

the support agent does not understand. On the other hand, I think it's a problem that experts [support agents] sometimes talk too 'complicated'. They speak 'IT language' and thereby eventually lose users. The user then has the problem that he cannot follow the support agent's walkthrough. [...]"

In the second part of the interview, the users were asked to think of a solution that would help reduce the identified communication problems. The requirements elicited are presented in the next section.

Solution Requirements and Suggestions. Respondent B suggests that there should be a manual instructing users how to explain their problems to the support agents, so they can provide a fast solution and give the best possible advice. Respondent B draws upon this and suggests placing a help-button on each webpage. Clicking the button would notify support agents that there is a problem with the specific site visited:

"And depending on which site you are browsing, you would be routed directly to the employee who is responsible. [...] this prevents that redundant information is requested."

Using a text field, portal users could provide additional information. A ticket could be automatically created and the support agent could phone the portal user as he knows his/her username. Respondent A further suggests that the button could also be used to send feedback whenever users think things could be simplified. He highlights the promptness of the solution:

"Sure, one could also do that by email, but that's more effort, since you have to explain again what you did before, etc. And that, for me, would be already too much work. But with the button—it should open a popup with a small text field—it would be much more comfortable."

Similar feedback services that allow end-users to share their ideas, praise, problems, and questions are provided by fast-growing startups such as Get Satisfaction[11] and User Voice[12].

11 http://getsatisfaction.com

12 http://uservoice.com/

3.1.4 Summary

The major issues identified in the case study include problems arising from a lack of shared visual context that result in misinterpretation in the communication. Users find it difficult to explain their problem and support agents struggle giving walkthrough instructions to users. The matter is further complicated by the language barrier (e.g., use of technical vocabulary) between the parties involved. Furthermore, lead users stress the importance of prompt responses. Support agents have recognized the need for sharing screens, but complain about compatibility issues with existing tools. The suggestions given by the respondents and the requirements elicited from the interview are used to set the design goals in the following section.

3.2 Design Goals

The challenge faced is not to extend the functionality of existing collaboration software, but to significantly reduce the conditions for entry to collaboration environments. Access should be possible from any browser-enabled device thus allowing real-time collaboration to be applied in new contexts, such as the live support scenario described in the previous section.

This ultimately allows multi-user access to existing browser-based applications. In summary, the design goals lay a foundation for a new generation of browser-based real-time collaboration tools supporting highly synchronous activities.

3.2.1 Functional Requirements

The collaboration service to be designed must allow multiple participants to synchronously share browser contents. Modifications of these contents made by any of the actors must be visible to all other participants in real-time. Furthermore, the co-browsing systems should provide the following common features of existing co-browsing solutions:

- page-push, i.e., navigating other participants to a specific Web address;
- co-navigation, e.g., clicking on a link in one browser seamlessly synchronizes the page loads across all browsers;

- co-scrolling, e.g., collaboratively scrolling the viewport of a website;
- co-form-filling, e.g., collaboratively editing Web forms including text fields, drop down lists, check boxes, radio buttons, and others;
- session handover, e.g., forwarding the state of a secure Web session to third parties.

3.2.2 Non-functional Requirements

The predominant goal is to provide a simple, fast, and secure way to allow ad hoc collaboration on arbitrary Web contents in real-time. In contrast to current approaches, Web access and the use of a modern browser should be the only requirements necessary. The use of the collaboration service should be transparent without requiring any technical effort by the end users. It should be lightweight, i.e., completely functional on a browser-native platform, thereby realizing the corresponding benefits of deployment illustrated in Table 2-1:

No Configuration. Using only prevailing Web standards, the service should be interoperable across organizational boundaries without requiring any configuration of the browser, the network or the firewall.

No Download. It should not be necessary to download third-party access programs that run outside the browser.

No Installation. Additional software or browser extensions should not be required.

No Footprint. The client systems used to collaborate should not be modified and no files should remain on the client system when collaboration ends.

In addition to the non-functional requirements targeted on ease of deployment, the following design aspects must be considered:

Scalability. To decrease the complexity of the collaboration environment it is crucial to design a lightweight server that manages the synchronization in a simple and efficient way. Reducing the state information that needs to be handled by the server allows moving load to clients and makes the collaboration scalable.

Real-time. As there are fuzzy interpretations of real-time communication, a more precise definition is required. Communication on the Web is said to be real-time when users see their own changes and that from others instantaneously without having to explicitly request them. For example when filling in Web forms, the text should be transmitted character by character as it is typed and be displayed synchronously on the screens of all participants.

To further specify the real-time architecture, the "*modes of communication model*" is used. This model describes the functional relationship and communication flow between users and the collaboration software (Dix 1998, p. 465): The change to the shared artifact must be visible to the acting user (feedback) and the remote users (feedthrough) in an instant. In particular, it is crucial to provide a solid infrastructure that allows quick feedback also for users that are affected by nondeterministic communication latency. As Sun and Chen (2002) state, reducing latency is important from a usability perspective, because many users subconsciously base their perception of the quality of the system rather on responsiveness than on functionality. The authors hence contend that poor responsiveness decreases the system's effectiveness in supporting collaborative work.

The following section deals with the architectural options for building a technical infrastructure that can be used to create real-time collaboration tools solely based on features natively supported by the current generation of Web browsers.

3.3 Architectural Options

The overall objective is to design an architecture, which provides a solid foundation to appropriately support high interactivity during synchronous collaboration sessions. One design decision to be made is whether user actions that modify the shared website are to be executed locally on the client or remotely on a central server. Figure 3-1 visualizes these architectural alternatives. While both architecture styles seem feasible, it is necessary to discuss their adequacy with regard to the aforementioned design goals. The centralized approach depicted on the left side of the figure is also referred to as the traditional client/server paradigm. The business logic is implemented on the server-side. Client functionality is limited to input and output operations. After each modification, clients have to update their local view with the server. The advantage of this approach is that changes are performed at a central location, making consistency control easier. Although change requests can be sent using

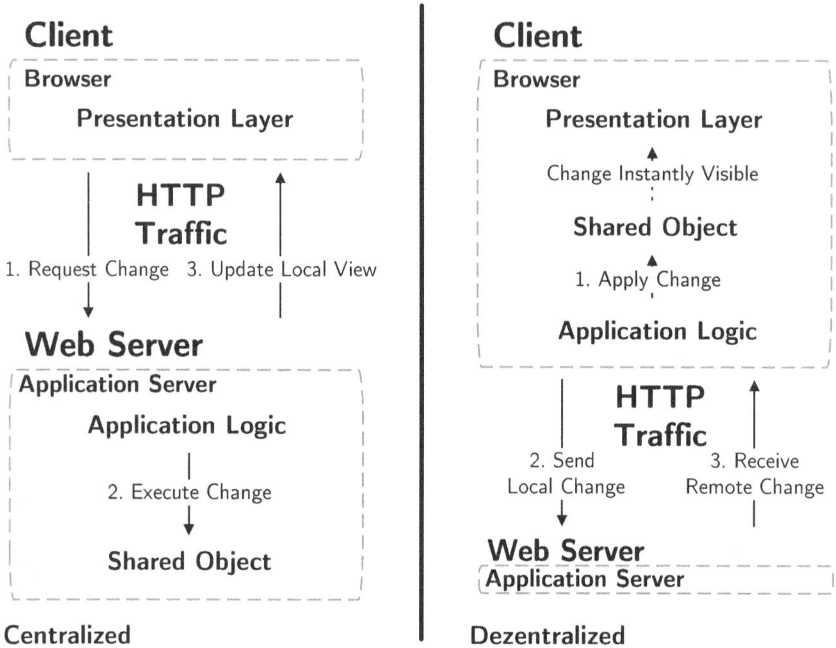

Figure 3-1: Architectural Alternatives

AJAX requests without interrupting user activity, this approach is to be evaluated critically with regard to the system's responsiveness. The availability of resources, such as CPU and memory restricts the scalability of this approach. With increasing load, the server quickly becomes a bottle neck. Additionally, the time delay between sending a change request (1.) and receiving the updated view (3.) negatively affects the performance. This style of blocking access to the shared object is also labeled pessimistic locking.

Increased processing capabilities of modern Web browsers allow moving the business logic—partially or entirely—to the client as demonstrated in the right part of the figure. The decentralized approach is also referred to as thin-server architecture (e.g., Pietschmann, Waltsgott, and Meißner 2010). For instance, many Web applications nowadays process data on the server, but use client-side functionality to filter and transform processed data. If the complete application state information is managed on the client side, the scalability can be improved significantly. As the business logic completely resides on the client side, changes to the shared object can be executed as decentralized updates or using a replication approach. When a collaborative session starts, every client is initialized with a copy of the shared object representing the current session state. Keeping state information in memory and repeatedly distributing the shared object to multiple clients is not required. All change operations can then be executed locally, thus minimizing network traffic and guaranteeing a faster response to user events. Lukosch and Schümmer (2007) recommend the use of a replication approach[13] when the degree of interactivity is high and the collaboration partners frequently invoke change operations on the shared object. To achieve low latency and high responsiveness in line with the real-time design goal, this approach is adopted as the most appropriate communication architecture for the prototype design.

3.4 Collaboration Proxy

Several challenges have to be mastered that prevented the design of a real-time collaboration services in the past. Overcoming the same-origin policy (SOP), which has been the major limiting factor in many state-of-the-art applications, is subject in this section. Subsequently, the structure and impact of the SOP is discussed and elaborated. Focus is put on the architectural design of a special collaboration proxy that overcomes the limitations.

3.4.1 Same-origin Policy

The SOP is a security feature enforced by browsers (IETF 2011). It prevents scripts embedded in Web documents from accessing resources loaded from another origin. Resources are defined to have the same origin if the protocol, domain, and port match. The idea behind this policy is to prevent any interaction between unrelated Web resources. This is fatal when designing collaboration functionality: In order to synchronize activities in the browser it is necessary to access and monitor Web content delivered via third-party servers.

The SOP applies to document operations, AJAX, and Cookies. As an exception, the SOP allows resources specified in `<script>` or `<iframe>` tags to be loaded across origin. In fact, inline frames are often used to load and display Web resources from different domains inside a single

13 They distinguish between *decentralized updates* and *decentralized objects*.

webpage. This technique is found in Web mash-ups. The mash-up iGoogle[14], for instance, aggregates contents, such as headlines from news websites, weather forecasts, and other widgets—all loaded from different origins. The same technique can be used when loading a shared website in the collaboration service. Many existing co-browsing services and research prototypes that only support URL-push functionality (see section 2.1.3) use this simple technique. Yet, the main problem remains unsolved: In order to provide a better and richer user experience, synchronization of user interactions and content of shared websites is required. Therefore, the SOP restrictions need to be bypassed.

3.4.2 Proxy Architecture

In order to overcome the SOP and enable cross-origin access, all resources must appear to originate from the same domain. All HTTP traffic needs to be intercepted to achieve this target. Although this may lead to performance limitations, it seems to be the only way of providing a cross-browser compatible way of overcoming the SOP. In the following, existing approaches of dynamically rerouting HTTP traffic are discussed. Afterwards, ways of adapting or extending these approaches for use in the context of collaborative browsing are evaluated.

Intermediate proxies act as mediators fulfilling gateway functionality by requesting remote resources and passing them on—with possible modifications and processing—to the clients. Standard Web proxies are such intermediate proxies. They are often used for caching purposes, speeding up Web access, or circumventing regional restrictions (Luotonen 1998). It is important to note that traditional Web proxy servers have to be configured manually by adjusting the appropriate settings of the Web browser and thereby sending all requests through the proxy. This contradicts the design goals (see section 3.2.2), as no client-side configuration should be required.

A rather novel approach is used by so-called Web service-based proxies or form-based proxies and has become popular in the context of anonymous browsing. To allow a smooth and unobtrusive browsing experience, Web service-based proxies perform a special processing on retrieved resources, so that all requests continue to activate the Web service proxy on subsequent requests. The benefit lies in easier deployment because

14 `http://www.google.de/ig`

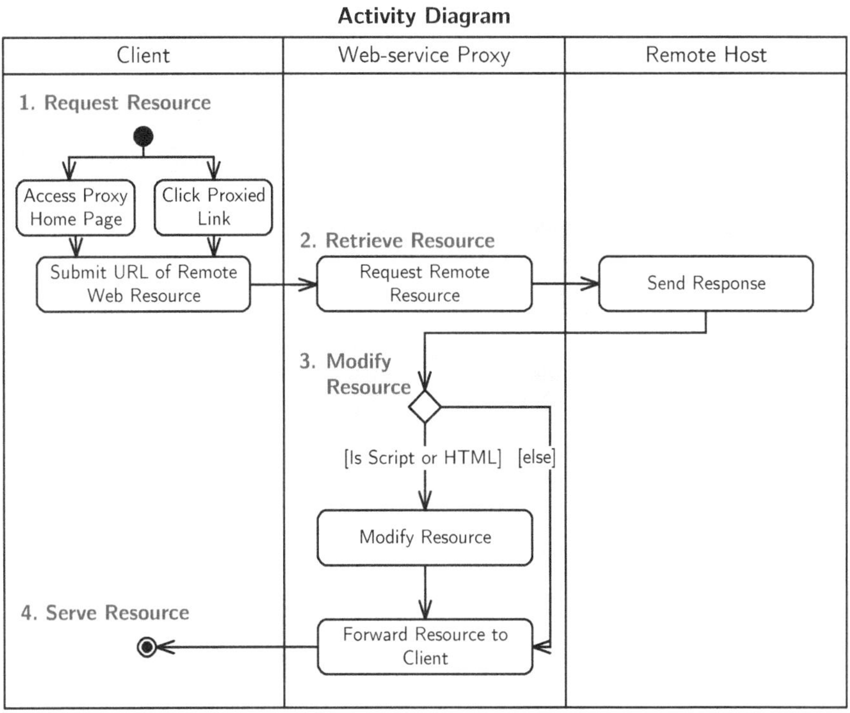

Figure 3-2: Web Service-based Content Adaption

these types of proxies require no client-side browser configuration (Leavitt 2009). Additionally, Web service-based proxies are more flexible than a traditional HTTP proxy because they can be reached by users inside firewalls. End users are relieved of the administrative burden to manually modify the systems proxy settings. Figure 3-2 illustrates the process of initiating a Web service-based proxy session:

Step (1)–Request Resource. There are two ways of starting a proxy session. Either clients simply access the proxy provider's home page and submit the URL they want to visit or they click on a link to a proxied page. Assuming that the intention is a visit to the website hosted at `http:// www.example.com`, the proxy URL could be:

`http://proxy.com/?url=http://www.example.com`

Step (2)–Retrieve Resource. In both cases the destination URL is passed to a Web service, which retrieves the requested page from a remote host. The server establishes an HTTP connection to the remote host using the same request method that is used in the request received (GET/POST). The proxy then downloads the requested resource from the server.

Step (3)–Modify Resource. To ensure subsequent requests are automatically redirected via the proxy, all resources that might trigger additional requests must be modified, before being passed back to the client. The proxy identifies relevant resources by inspecting the `Content-Type` header field of the response received from the remote host. If the `Content-Type` indicates either a (Java)Script or HTML resource (e.g., `text/html`, `text/javascript`, `text/css`), the resource is parsed and modified. Static resources, such as image files, remain unmodified and are directly forwarded to the client. The modification process aims at redirecting all HTTP traffic initiated by the Web resource, so that future requests will point to the Web service proxy instead of the original Web host. Additionally, measures have to be taken in order to ensure that Web resources are loaded into the correct target windows. For instance, page requests may be triggered from within the shared webpage and specify the target frame using relative references, such as `top` (topmost frame), `parent` (parent frame), or `blank` (new window). The references top and parent would result in the shared webpage to overwrite and unload the parent frame that controls synchronization. Therefore, the collaboration proxy has to rewrite the target of all links and form elements to point to the synchronized frame instead of the top or parent frame. When pages are loaded in a new, i.e. blank window, the synchronization service has to recognize this and take care of synchronizing this additional window.

Modification of Web resources subsumes techniques such as rewriting hyperlinks and redirecting AJAX and other network requests initiated by the JavaScript engine. Although this task is straightforward, the implementation is not trivial. Decisions have to be made as to which resources to cache and how to submit form data. More advanced techniques include reassigning cookies and modifying HTTP headers.

Step (4)–Serve Resource. Finally, the resource is served back to the client and rendered by the browser. Although the document originates from a remote host, it is received via the mediating synchronization proxy. This approach is in line with the same-origin policy, avoids cross-site scripting issues, and hence overcomes the same domain limitations of the work presented by Esenther (2002a) and Lowet and Goergen (2009). Once received, client browsers can load the returned HTML code into an iframe. To the browser, both the synchronization scripts and the content frame seem to originate from the same domain. Hence, synchronization scripts from parent frames are allowed to handle and intercept events occurring in the Document Object Model of the iframe.

The crucial factor impacting on the reliability and performance of Web service-based proxies, however, lies in the implementation of robust techniques for the modification of the resource in Step (3). These are discussed in section 4.3.2.

3.5 Real-time Communication

A typical challenge in collaborative multi-user applications is the synchronization of local states on all clients. Therefore, the exchange of messages between clients is necessary. Passing messages through an intermediate server is required, since client-to-client communication is not possible via the HTTP protocol. Direct communication between client systems could be realized by installing Web servers on each "*client system*" (Mehra, Grundy, and Hosking 2004), however, this approach would contradict the objective of providing a lightweight, easy to deploy, and flexible architecture. Other previous attempts to add such functionality have involved extension mechanisms such as browser plug-ins, Java applets, and proprietary protocols, e.g., FlashXML sockets or Java RMI. Realizing collaboration functionality on the basis of the stateless HTTP protocol, optimized for client requests, is challenging. To be applicable in the context of synchronous collaboration, the HTTP protocol must allow for the server to send notifications to the clients.

3.5.1 Request/Response Paradigm

In order to replicate changes in a decentralized environment (see section 3.3), it is necessary to propagate locally executed user actions to other clients. The HTTP protocol, which is used as the transport layer for communication, is built upon the request/response paradigm.

It provides a one direction half-duplex mode communication that is inefficient for modern event-driven applications and services. All communication has to be initiated by the client. Any server-side response has to be preceded by a client-side request. Although interactivity has increased in Web 2.0 applications, there is no simple way of sending events from the server to the clients. Because of this limitation, the HTTP protocol was

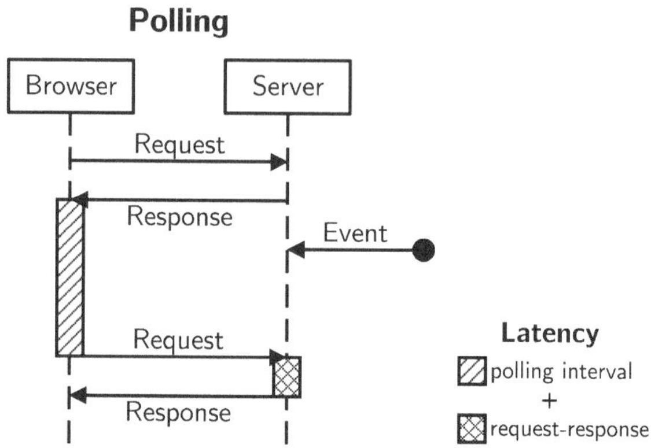

Figure 3-3: HTTP 1.0 Client Polling

not used for implementing synchronous collaboration. In his paper concerning the challenges of web-based collaboration, Dix (1997, p. 143) states: "*HTTP is certainly not suited to real-time conversations!*"

There is a variety of approaches that aim to overcome this limitation and enable the server to send notifications to the clients. Scalability and latency are important criteria for assessing the efficiency of those approaches (Sun and D. Chen 2002). Latency is measured as the delay between the occurrence of events on the server and the receipt of a notification by the client.

3.5.2 Polling

Polling is one approach of retrieving remote event notifications and is commonly used due to its ease of implementation. The client continuously sends requests to the server. Upon receiving the response from the server, the connection is closed and a new request is issued by the client. The idle time between receiving a response from the server and sending a new request is called the polling interval (Crane and McCarthy 2008). While interruptions of user activity can be avoided by using AJAX, the polling approach still has serious drawbacks. In the worst case, a server-side event occurs immediately after sending a response. As depicted in Figure 3-3, in this case, latency equals the sum of the polling interval plus the time that passes until the HTTP response of the last polling request has reached the client. Hence, one critical decision when using this approach is how to choose the length of the polling interval. In case the interval is too long, the client might receive critical notifications late.

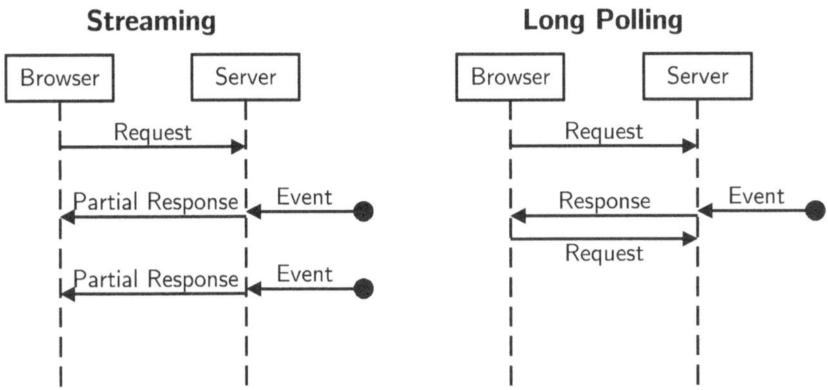

Figure 3-4: HTTP 1.1 Server Push Alternatives

Conversely, scalability is reduced and the network load increased when the interval is too short. As can be seen, the maintenance of a polling connection can introduce significant bandwidth consumption and overhead.

Innovative techniques use new features introduced in the HTTP 1.1 standard (Fielding et al. 1999). They enable the server to establish persistent connections and send event notifications over HTTP to clients with negligible latency. These notifications can be sent in response to occurring events without explicit polling. According to the outdated HTTP 1.0 standard, the connection to the server had to be closed after each request-response cycle (Berners-Lee, Fielding, and Frystyk 1996). Only the latest HTTP 1.1 standard allows keeping the connection alive, thus enabling faster communication. With HTTP 1.1, there are two options to implement server-side client notifications with low latency: Streaming and Long Polling.

3.5.3 Streaming

Streaming uses a so-called "*forever response.*" In contrast to polling, the connection is not closed after sending a message from the server. This way, several messages can be sent in a data stream over a single HTTP connection (multi-part/chunked response). Following this approach, latency is minimal because different polling clients can be notified immediately after the event has occurred as depicted on the left part of Figure 3-4. The lag is solely determined by the time the HTTP response needs to reach the client. One significant disadvantage of streaming is that it is not possible to recognize whether a given client is still receiving messages. Since the HTTP response is sent in parts, there is a risk that messages received are delayed, because they might be buffered by proxy servers. This might lead to a state in which the server is still sending messages although the client is already disconnected.

3.5.4 Long Polling

A compromise between polling and streaming is long polling. This approach utilizes a so-called persistent or long-lived HTTP connection. Connections to the server are kept open until either a server-side event or a timeout occurs. In both cases, the client has to send a new HTTP request to the server after receiving the response. Using this strategy, long polling preserves the low latency of the HTTP streaming approach and at the same time avoids several disadvantages of both streaming and traditional polling, respectively. The frequency of sending empty responses is reduced because the server does not send responses immediately after a request has been received. By forcing the client to send a new request after a message has been received, it can be ensured that all clients are still active. This is illustrated on the right part of Figure 3-4.

3.5.5 WebSockets

Adhering to Web standards, real-time message exchange between client and server is only feasible by enhancing the traditional request-response paradigm using the techniques outlined above. However, server push technologies are subject to ongoing development and enhancement. HTML 5 WebSockets are one of the foundations for the next-generation web and are expected to facilitate the use of the Web as a platform for the development of collaborative applications. The Web Hypertext Technology Working Group is responsible for the specification of HTML 5 and defines the full-duplex WebSocket communication model (WHATWG 2009). The idea is to allow bidirectional Web communication using a standardized HTTP-based WebSocket protocol. Deploying WebSockets must be supported by the client and the server. In today's server infrastructure the use of WebSockets is not yet feasible: Although prototypical implementations available for the server side exist, support on the browser side is lacking. At the time of writing, the WebSocket implementation could only be tested successfully on Google Chrome v4+, Apple Safari v5+ and Mozilla Firefox v6+.

3.5.6 Restrictions

Due to the thread-per-request model used by traditional Web servers, the server push approaches outlined in the previous section are not scalable and thus inapplicable for collaborative sessions with many participants. In a thread-per-request architecture each request from a client is handled in a separate thread on the server. For instance, a Java Web container allocates a dedicated servlet thread for each incoming request. Servicing a new client request reserves one thread which blocks one socket until the response is transmitted to the client (Hu, Pyarali, and D. C. Schmidt 1997). This is why the thread-per-request model is also referred to as blocking input/output. Traditionally, it has been the best solution for dealing with many concurrent client requests allowing content to be delivered as fast as possible. The underlying assumption was that content either is available on the Web server in an instant or it can be quickly retrieved from a database, hence minimizing the number of blocking threads in memory.

This assumption does not hold true for the event-driven collaboration architecture employed by the designed prototype. When a client asks the server to be notified of an event, the response content cannot be retrieved like a resource, but is generated by a remote party at an unpredictable time with an unknown frequency. Keeping this in mind, each participant in a co-browsing session would have one request open to the server, waiting to be informed about other users' actions. Most of these requests would merely be idle. As a consequence, blocking connections would consume all memory available on the server and thus limit its scalability. Therefore, it is apparent that the way traditional Web servers process requests is not suited to real-time collaboration scenarios.

As a solution, an increasing number of modern Web servers such as Tomcat, Glassfish, and Jetty allow programmers to use non-blocking input/output (NIO) to account for the special demands of asynchronous request processing in an event-driven architecture. NIO allows suspending HTTP requests without consuming or blocking resources. The thread can then be used to process another request. Thus, a request can enter a waiting state and be resumed when an asynchronous event or a predefined timeout occurs. The need to support asynchronous HTTP processing on the server-side has also been recognized in the Java Community. JSR-315 is an attempt to bring asynchronous processing to the upcoming Servlet 3.0 standard. To achieve a highly scalable architecture, the non-blocking continuations of the Jetty Web server (Wilkins 2008) are used for implementing the prototype.

3.6 Synchronization Strategy

As mentioned before, many screen sharing approaches use continuous image-streaming to transfer browser contents. In some cases, a simple mouse click can refresh the entire browser window or start an animation. If image data is sent, network traffic will be unacceptably high. Taking into account that most of today's Internet connections are asynchronous with only limited upload bandwidth, a synchronization strategy that minimizes data transmission is particularly favorable. Such synchronization strategies enable multiple users to concurrently work on the same application without having to pass input control to each other.

In order to achieve this it is necessary to take advantage of the browser's structure. For instance, existing traditional co-browsing solutions use the simplest form of synchronization by replicating the URL of the content displayed in the browser (see section 2.1.3).

To preserve the shared objects' consistency, however, it is necessary to also synchronize changes to the content as the user interacts with it. Providing a robust solution that works in a cross-browser manner without plug-ins is a problem that remains unsolved by existing research. Finding an approach that minimizes network traffic and allows high-performance communication by replicating incremental changes between clients is highly desirable. To be able to identify a solid solution, it is crucial to understand how browsers handle user interactions. A high-level browser structure is given in the next section.

3.6.1 Browser High-level Structure

The browser's major task is to retrieve Web resources and present them to the user. Although Web resources can have numerous types, using HTML rather than image or pure text data is the standard. HTML markup, once loaded from the network, is parsed by the browser's rendering engine and represented within a logical structure called Document Object Model (DOM). The DOM has been specified and promoted by the World Wide Web Consortium (W3C 2004) in order to enhance functionality and interoperability of the Web. Although not all vendors fully comply with the specification, the high level structure described here applies to all browsers.

The DOM represents the content, structure, and style of an HTML Web resource. It is a hierarchical tree containing every element in an HTML

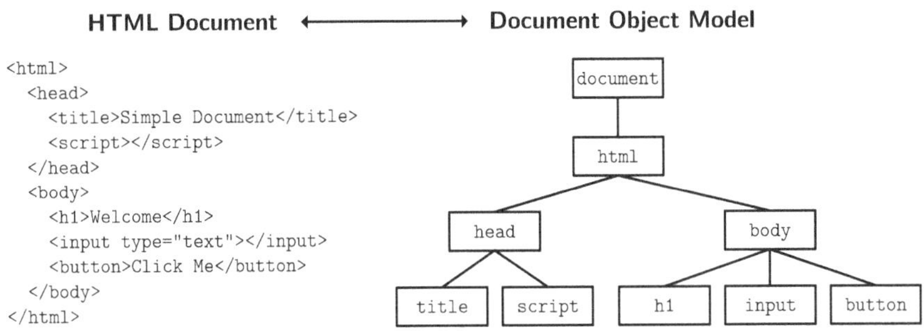

Figure 3-5: Representation of HTML Documents in Browsers

document. Each tag in the HTML markup is turned into a node in the DOM tree. This simplified flow is illustrated in Figure 3-5. The DOM tree provides an object representation of the HTML markup and thereby offers a programmatic interface for dynamic access and manipulation of the content, structure, and style of HTML documents. Nodes and their properties can be read, added, updated, and deleted using JavaScript.

JavaScript events are generated by the browser engine when the user interacts with the Web content. User actions result in corresponding events being dispatched on the currently focused node in the DOM tree. According to the DOM specification, these events are categorized in `KeyEvents` (e.g., `keydown`, `keyup`, `keypress`), `MouseEvents` (e.g., `click`, `mousemove`, `mouseover`), and `UIEvents` (`focus`, `blur`, `resize`). By default, the event travels up the tree until event handlers on all parent nodes have been triggered. This event propagation feature can be leveraged to monitor user actions. Typically user actions are reflected as a change on the UI implying a change in the DOM tree. For instance, pressing keys when the focus is on the input field would invoke the `keypress` event handler on the input node and display the typed characters on the UI and at the same time changing the `value` property of the node.

With respect to the way the browser operates, two alternatives seem feasible to incrementally replicate state changes in a decentralized environment. Assuming that participants are displaying the same URL in their browsers, local states can be synchronized by replicating:

1. changes to the shared webpage, reflected in the state of DOM tree, or

2. user events triggering these state changes.

In the following sections, both synchronization approaches are discussed regarding their specific benefits and drawbacks.

3.6.2 Synchronization of DOM Tree Changes

Assuming all browsers have been initialized by loading the same URL, the DOM tree State in all browsers should be the same. Keeping participants' browsers synchronized would require monitoring the DOM tree for changes and then replicating these changes. Upon receiving a change notification, other browsers can access and modify their DOM trees accordingly, thereby synchronizing UIs. For instance a node inserted in the DOM tree can easily be serialized and sent to another browser. Using the JavaScript DOM interface, the node can be inserted at the specified location updating the local state.

A major disadvantage of this approach lies in the fact that only UI changes are replicated. User actions that trigger a state change in the client-side business logic of the Web application are not reflected in the UI and thus not transmitted. As a result, subsequent actions performed by other users will not lead to the intended result.

Prototypically implementing this architecture showed that, additionally, browsers may build different DOM trees from ill-formed HTML markup. This is especially the case when not adhering to the strict XHTML standard and omitting closing tags. The problem was encountered testing the markup in Mozilla Firefox 3.0 and Microsoft Internet Explorer 8.0. Although creating more overhead, this problem alone would not be an obstacle for the usage of this replication strategy. By injecting unique id attributes to the markup before passing it to the clients, nodes can still be uniquely identified even if they are placed at different positions in the DOM tree.

This limits the co-browsing experience to static websites or dynamic applications that do not use local state information. Co-browsing modern dynamic Web applications becomes limited to the presenter/viewer paradigm.

3.6.3 Synchronization of User Events

Collaborative activity can be represented by the occurrence of browser events caused by user actions. Each user action invokes an event handler with an event object supplying all information necessary to replicate the

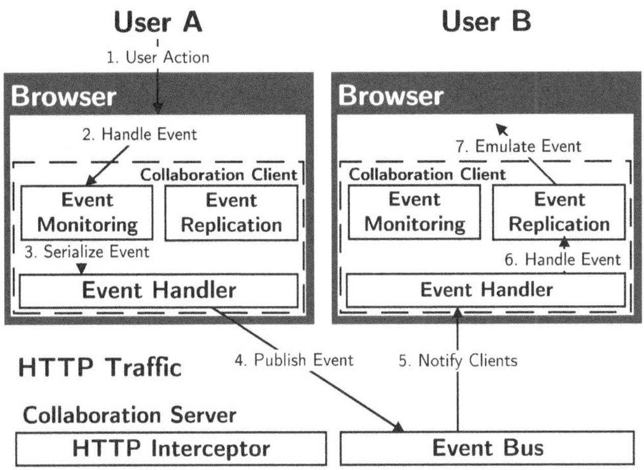

Figure 3-6: Event Synchronization

event. For instance, text input fields trigger `keypress` events when characters are entered. The same way mouse click events can be monitored. Registering and replicating these events across all browsers enables a shared synchronized view for all participants.

In order to make an event-based synchronization service work, a monitoring script has to be inserted into the webpage which captures and subsequently publishes events. Notifications of user actions (mouse and keyboard events) can then be intercepted and synchronized among all clients (see Figure 3-6).

The client executing a change operation on the shared Web content (1., 2.) notifies the server of the actions carried out (3., 4.). The server subsequently propagates the message to all participating clients (5.). Finally, all clients replicate the user event on their local copy of the shared Web document (6., 7.). This replication strategy requires pushing the local state to each new client joining a running session. The local state comprises not only the current state of the shared artifact, but also additional collaboration-related information such as elements being locked by users.

3.6.4 Session Handover

To join a meeting the participants need to access the service via the same ticket number, which is equivalent to a session ID and can be encoded in a clickable URL and sent via email or instant messaging services. Alternatively, the ID can be entered directly on a webpage provided by the collaboration server.

A client joining an existing session has to be initialized with the state information of the current session. Therefore, it is necessary to design a technique that enables stateful session handover. The session handover must occur seamless and function across heterogeneous devices, such as smartphones, tablets, netbooks, etc.

As the collaboration proxy mediates all HTTP traffic between client and remote host, it might seem to be an easy task to retrieve the current URL of the document shared in the collaborative session and forward it to joining clients. However, HTML documents can be nested in structure. A parent document may define a set of child documents also referred to as a set of frames. In this case, loading the parent document triggers additional HTTP requests, each of which returns a document with the mime type text/html. Upon forwarding the request, the intercepting proxy does not know the structure of the HTML document and hence cannot identify the document representing the last state change. For example, after sequentially browsing two webpages (A, B) the state change should be: A $\rightarrow$ B. Assuming B is a nested document containing the subframes B1 and B2, the server would record the following incorrect state changes: A$\rightarrow$ B $\rightarrow$ B1 $\rightarrow$ B2. However, it should be A $\rightarrow$ B. To correctly detect the state change on the server-side would require parsing document B, which is an unacceptable overhead (Hsieh et al. 2006).

As it was a design goal to make the server as scalable as possible, the approach of managing state information on the server-side is not a valid option. Instead, the server is designed to be stateless. As a consequence, all session information needs to be retrieved from clients that already are participating in a shared session. Based on the replication of user operations, all local states can be assumed to be synchronous; therefore, it does not matter which existing client is chosen to provide the state. In a collaborative browsing session, the current state is represented by the state of the shared Web document, which can be specified by its URL, its cookies, and the value of unsubmitted input fields. If the shared website is comprised of multiple frames, this information has to be retrieved and serialized for all documents.

The sequence diagram in Figure 3-7 illustrates the conceptual design of the solution approach. Depicted is the case where client A joins an existing session of client B and client C. Client A creates a buffer (1.), in

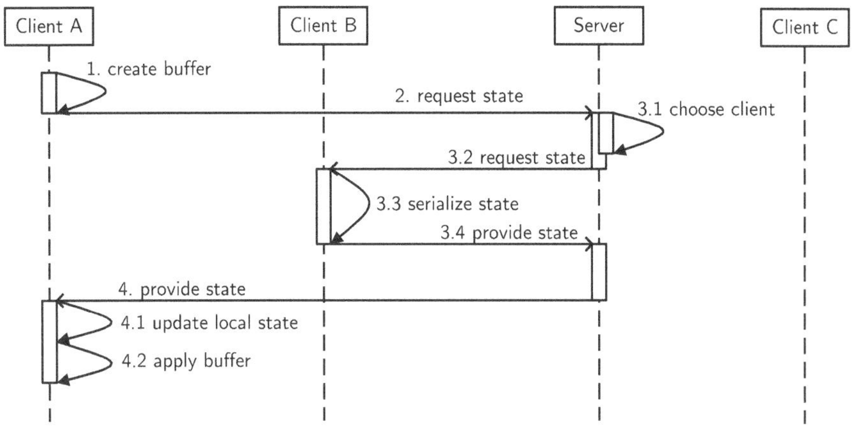

Figure 3-7: Session Handover

order to cache incoming messages for the duration of the state request. This is to ensure that no user operation is lost between request (2.) and receipt (3.1, 3.2, 3.3, 3.4) of the current state. To provide a better insight, this case is depicted in a second diagram. Upon receiving a state request (2.), the server randomly chooses a participating client (3.1) and forwards the request (3.2). Now the randomly selected client B (3.3) serializes its local state and sends it back to the server (3.4). The server eventually forwards the serialized state to the joining client (4.1). The client then updates its local state by deserializing the received data and then processing the buffer of cached user operations (4.2). Using server-initiated event notification as described above is one of the technical challenges; it has been implemented using browser-native functionality only.

Complementary to the previous sequence diagram, Figure 3-8 illustrates the use of the buffer, which caches the change operations received during request and receipt of the session state (2.1-2.3). Having received the updated state (1.2), client A can reconstruct the change operations contained in the buffer that are not yet reflected within the local state and can update the state accordingly (1.3-1.4).

3.6.5 Concurrency Control

The central challenges in designing the collaboration functionality are maintaining a consistent view and coordinating concurrent access to the so-called shared object. Working on tasks concurrently via the Web

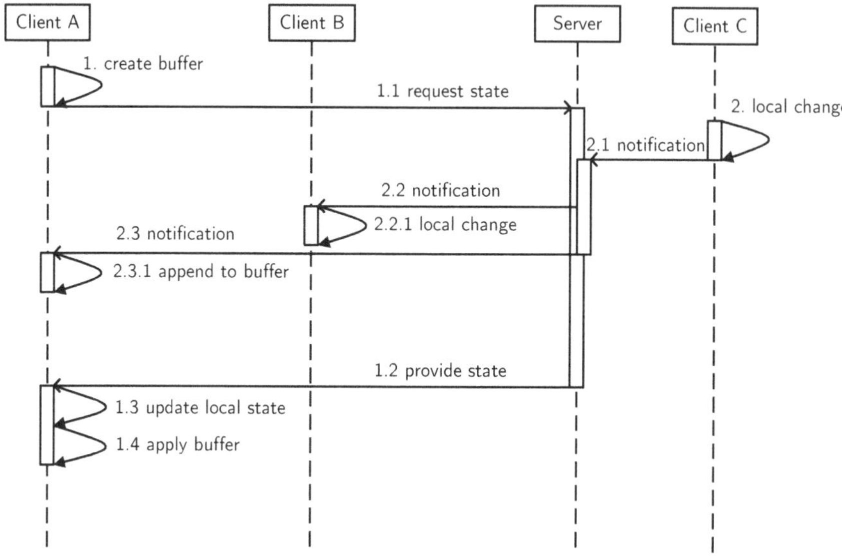

Figure 3-8: Buffering Change Operations

requires a high degree of coordination. One fundamental challenge of coordinating access to shared artifacts in real-time applications is ensuring that each user action yields the desired result on all clients. This concept is referred to as intension preservation (Bo et al. 2004). It ensures the consistency of the shared object.

If event synchronization is unconstrained, interference between clients is inevitable. It is likely that two or more users try to modify the same element at the same time. Error free access can only be guaranteed when interferences between actors are avoided (Locking) or resolved (Operational Transformation). Mechanisms aiming to avoid or resolve such conflicts are discussed in papers concerning concurrency control and are subsumed below.

Realizing concurrency control is a well-known problem in the context of CSCW. In fact, many frameworks provide collaborative functionality in form of reusable components. These components support developers by handling all collaboration-specific challenges and problems like synchronization of client states and concurrency control. Examples for such frameworks are DreamTeam (Roth and Unger 1998), COAST (J. Schümmer and Schuckmann 2000) and DyCE (Tietze and Rubart 2001). While frameworks encapsulate technical details and facilitate implementation, they also restrict developers by imposing a certain programming language or a special class structure. Additionally, frameworks are bound to specific technologies such as Java RMI. This inhibits the development of novel tools. Lukosch and Schümmer (2004) support this argument and recommend using design patterns instead. These approved patterns are independent of the technology used for realization. For the construction of the synchronite prototype a browser-native architecture and hence communication via the HTTP protocol form the basic infrastructure for implementing the collaboration support. Because of the novelty of the Web technologies used, design patterns rather than predefined frameworks will be applied for the artifact construction.

Real-time Web collaboration as provided by synchronite enables multiple participants to concurrently edit pre-existing Web documents originally designed for single users. To enable real-time concurrent modification of Web documents, an appropriate control mechanism is required.

Stefik et al. (1987) argue that it is not necessary to implement mechanisms that technically avoid interference. When two users by accident happen to edit the same data, both users would notice that the data is changed independently of the own actions. Greenberg and Marwood (1994) are of the opinion that it is sufficient when collaborators know that elements are being edited by other users. The idea that in the context of CSCW solely the consent among collaboration partners is sufficient to clarify conflicts is called reliance on *social protocols*. Based on an empirical study, Tse et al. (2004) state that actors collaborating in a so-called Single Display Groupware (SDG) naturally tend to avoid conflict situations when they are predictable. This is the case when the element in the shared environment is marked as being accessed by a specific user. Other studies show that despite the reliance on social protocols interferences can still occur in four percent of all user actions (Campbell 2004).

It is correct that trusting on social protocols helps to avoid conflicts in some situations. For instance, it might be considered impolite to delete work of other participants. However, relying on this rule only does not guarantee consistency. Even when all collaborators adhere to social protocols, interferences may still occur as a result of carelessness and a lack of attention. With less formalized team sessions like collaborative brainstorming this may not be a problem. When jointly editing Web forms in an online order process (see section 2.3), social protocols cannot be accepted as an appropriate mechanism for avoiding unwanted results. Campbell (2002b) confirms this view and discourages the use of this strategy for resolving conflicts when errors are not tolerable. Concurrency control strategies that allow multiple users access to a shared object and guarantee maintaining consistency at the same time can be classified as pessimistic and optimistic approaches.

The strictest pessimistic approach is the Floor Control Pattern. Since this method only grants writing permission on the shared workspace to one user at a time it is also referred to as Single Writer Multiple Reader pattern. Using this pattern is adequate in cases where parallel change operations have to be avoided. This can be intended for clarity reasons or when concurrent access to the resource is not possible. This approach is used by many screen sharing applications (see section 2.1.3), which limit input control to one user at a time. Prior to granting a participant access to a shared object it is checked whether the element has been locked by another user. This requires a round-trip to a central server.

Floor control avoids conflicts by restricting concurrent access, hence eliminating many benefits of synchronous collaboration. Because of this property, several authors rate floor control to be inappropriate. Moreover, locking the entire workspace is inefficient. Users that currently do not have access to the workspace may only watch and wait until the holder of input control has finished working. These situations happen more often when collaboration is part of an unstructured process, where the tasks do not follow a predefined workflow (J. Schümmer and Schuckmann 2000). Even though floor control is used in many research prototypes, it is not applicable in the context of real-time Web collaboration. To allow synchronous collaboration a strategy permitting concurrent access is required.

A more efficient concurrency control approach is pessimistic locking. In contrast to floor control, not the entire workspace, but specified parts are locked. The granularity level chosen determines the efficiency of this approach. In case it is too coarse, the number of activities that can be conducted in parallel is reduced. Fine-granular locking increases the number of parallel activities possible, but also increases the need for lock requests that have to be sent over the network. Before a local change request is executed, users have to wait for a round-trip to the central server. In an optimistic approach, local changes to a shared object are executed immediately without being blocked. Other participants are notified of this change. This improves the perceived responsiveness and makes optimistic approaches insensitive to network latencies. Maintaining consistency, however, requires the use of operational transformations to resolve conflicting update notifications (D. Nichols et al.

1995). Using operational transformations in turn requires the server to keep a copy of the shared artifact in memory during collaborative sessions. As it is a goal to keep the server thin and stateless, this approach is not considered appropriate.

Evaluating the above-mentioned shortcomings of social protocol, floor control, and pessimistic locking approaches, the pessimistic concurrency control strategy is identified as being the most adequate for use in collaborative browsing. To allow synchronous collaboration, it is deemed best to apply locking on the level of single HTML input elements. This allows multiple participants to collaboratively edit Web forms without interfering with each other (cf. functional requirement *co-form-filling* in section 3.2.1).

3.7 Security of Sensitive Information

Care has to be taken that security of the synchronized Web application is not breached by the collaboration layer or the collaborative activity. At first, it has to be ensured that traffic cannot be disrupted by third parties. Secondly, it has to be ensured that sensitive data is not replicated to other participants in the same session. Meeting these requirements allows guaranteeing security outside and within collaboration sessions.

Many Web servers use encrypted SSL communication channels to establish secure transactions. The synchronization mechanism must replicate one session to multiple participating browsers. To enable collaborative access to secure resources, it is necessary for the proxy server to act as a man-in-the-middle (cf. Callegati, Cerroni, and Ramilli 2009). The server has to establish one secure connection with the destination server and then replicate this secure connection to each client browser. To achieve this, the collaboration proxy needs to be able to deliver a valid SSL certificate signed by an accepted Certificate Authority (CA) to each client. The client browser accepts the signed certificate of the collaboration proxy and consequently establishes a secure SSL channel. The proxy itself receives and—if trusted—accepts the certificate delivered by the destination server. Using this technique guarantees confidentiality of data.

Engaging in collaboration always means sharing a common view and therefore exposing potentially confidential or security-relevant information to all participants. To facilitate the adoption of the novel collaboration service, there must be confidence that sensitive information is protected and no security violation is caused by collaborative activity. It has to be ensured, that

(1) participants do not gain access to data that is not explicitly shared and that

(2) sensitive information such as passwords or credit card information is not replicated.

Issue (1) is rooted in the fact that traditional collaboration software has access to the complete file system and all screen contents. Profound trust is required towards the vendors of such software and collaboration partners. Actors must be confident that granted access rights are not abused. The browser-native architecture technically eliminates the chance of exposing any sensitive information stored outside of the shared Web document. The browser's secure sandbox improves security as an additional line of defense compared to traditional collaboration software.

Issue (2) describes the need to provide additional security by restricting the transmission of sensitive data even inside collaborative sessions. To account for this concern, input to password fields is not synchronized by default. Additionally, the collaboration layer can be configured to excluding other input fields from being transmitted to remote participants.

3.8 Multi-user Awareness

An essential difference between single and multiuser applications is the need to inform the participants on all occurring events that result from the collaboration context (see section 2.1.2). Awareness information is needed for each participant to coordinate his/her own activities. This exchange of status and context information is referred to as Workspace Awareness (Gutwin and Greenberg 2002). Supporting the awareness of all participants has been shown to improve the usability of real-time collaboration systems (B. Jiang, J. Yang, and Arabnia 2006). With regard to the collaboration service to be designed this means that each user should be able to recognize when other users access the shared Web document and which modifications they make. Implicit and explicit communication as well as a list of all meeting attendees is essential. A notification service that enables implicit information exchange between the attendees seems reasonable. This service informs all team members about operations conducted and makes it easier for all participants to perceive the changes made. All input elements of the Web document currently selected for data entry are visually highlighted.

3.8.1 Telepointer

Replicating mouse pointers on all participants' screens has been recognized as an important awareness feature (e.g., Graham 1997; Aoki 2002; Dyck et al. 2004; Bu et al. 2006) and is employed in many screen sharing applications. It helps participants to better interpret and anticipate other users' intentions and assimilate their gestures. Designing telepointer functionality for a browser-native collaboration system is subject to several challenges.

Network Latency and Jitter. Firstly, the quality of the network connection may inhibit the accuracy and smoothness of replicated mouse movements. This is particularly fatal as enabling real-time communication via HTTP requires some overhead. As a result of latency, the remote mouse pointer may appear slow. Additionally, jitter, the variation in latency of network connections, inevitably results in jumpy movement of telepointers. This impedes the ability of users to recognize remote users' actions. Existing research has targeted these problems by presenting various algorithms that ensure remote movements are replicated smoothly. These include quality of experience models (Dyck et al. 2004) and motion prediction schemes (B. Jiang et al. 2006). Reducing the effects of latency and jitter is a field thoroughly researched. Proven techniques can be applied in the prototype.

Dynamic Web Content. The second problem occurs as a result of the dynamic nature of the shared Web content. Due to different screen resolutions, the mouse pointer cannot be simply positioned at the same coordinates as on the source screen. Scaling the coordinates according to screen dimensions is a quick and simple solution usually applied to this problem. As the browser content is not homogeneously scaled, but subject to a complicated reflow process, items may be positioned at different coordinates. Elements are dynamically repositioned according to the browser's default settings and user-defined style sheets. Finally, even when all participants view the same webpage at the same resolution, elements may be positioned inconsistently because different browsers or language settings are used.

To overcome this issue, the position of the mouse pointer is not defined by coordinates relative to the browser screen, but relative to the DOM node it is positioned over. This ensures that the telepointer will be positioned over the correct node. As nodes might be scaled in size in other browsers, normalized relative coordinates have to be used. Capturing the mouse position is done according to the following algorithm:

1. Listen to mouse move events and identify the DOM node the pointer is positioned over.

2. Calculate the normalized vertical and horizontal offset relating to the top left corner of this element (scaled from 0...1).

3. Publish a node selector and the normalized relative coordinates to other browsers.

This allows telepointers to be positioned correctly independent of the way different browsers render the Web document. Finding an identifier for an HTML node that reliably locates the node across different browsers is difficult in real-world scenarios where malformed HTML code in nested tag structures results in different browsers applying different repair techniques and thereby constructing different DOM trees. As a result, the same node is located at different positions and might not be found when using the position in the DOM tree as a selector.

3.8.2 Chat

To supplement implicit communication, a chat is implemented as an additional means of exchanging information between participants. The chat enables instant messaging between participants, which increases usability as most users are already familiar with this style of communication (B. Jiang et al. 2006).

3.8.3 Typing Indicator

A well-known problem in remote communication is caused by the delay while waiting for other participants to respond. To increase multi-user awareness, a typing indicator is used.

The indicator displays information when a participant is typing a message in the chat window or editing an input field on a website. The chat typing indicator is particularly beneficial in support scenarios, as it allows to structure conversations in a coherent questions-answer style: A support agent can wait until a user has finished typing. At the same time, customers are kept aware of the assistance when support agents are typing longer messages. Additionally, the users are made aware of the immediate service.

3.9 Live Support Process

An important aspect of collaboration software is the integration into third-party websites such as online shops and Web portals. Being able to initiate an ad hoc support session at the click of a button is a crucial requirement in live support scenarios (see section 3.2.1). Although the design of the support process is based on a case study conducted with the helpdesk services of University of Mannheim, care has been taken to create a flexible solution that can easily be adapted to other environments. Figure 3-9 shows the live support process model as a UML activity diagram. For purpose of clarity, some activities and control flows were omitted, e.g., the customer or support agent can stop the support session at any time and resume it later. Moreover, a support session might include multiple users or multiple support agents. The process is divided in three stages, namely initiation, live support, and follow-up. The initiation stage is comprised of all activities leading to a collaborative session. Contact can be established by both the customer and the support agent. When the user browses the website and encounters a problem, he can request support by clicking on a live support button. The system automatically detects whether the user is logged on or not. In the first case, the support request is directly forwarded to the system. In the latter case, the user is asked to enter contact details first. Although omitted in the diagram, the user could additionally be asked to specify the reason for the request. This information can help to route the support request to the correct agent as suggested in the lead user interview (see section 3.1.3). The user is informed as soon as an agent becomes available and may then choose to confirm or reject the support request. This intermediate step can also be omitted. Delivering effective assistance also requires agents to be able to send support offers. In case users decide to contact the helpdesk via telephone, the support agent can still select the user in the web contact console and send a live support offer to the browser. The Web contact console is designed to be a central dashboard for support agents.

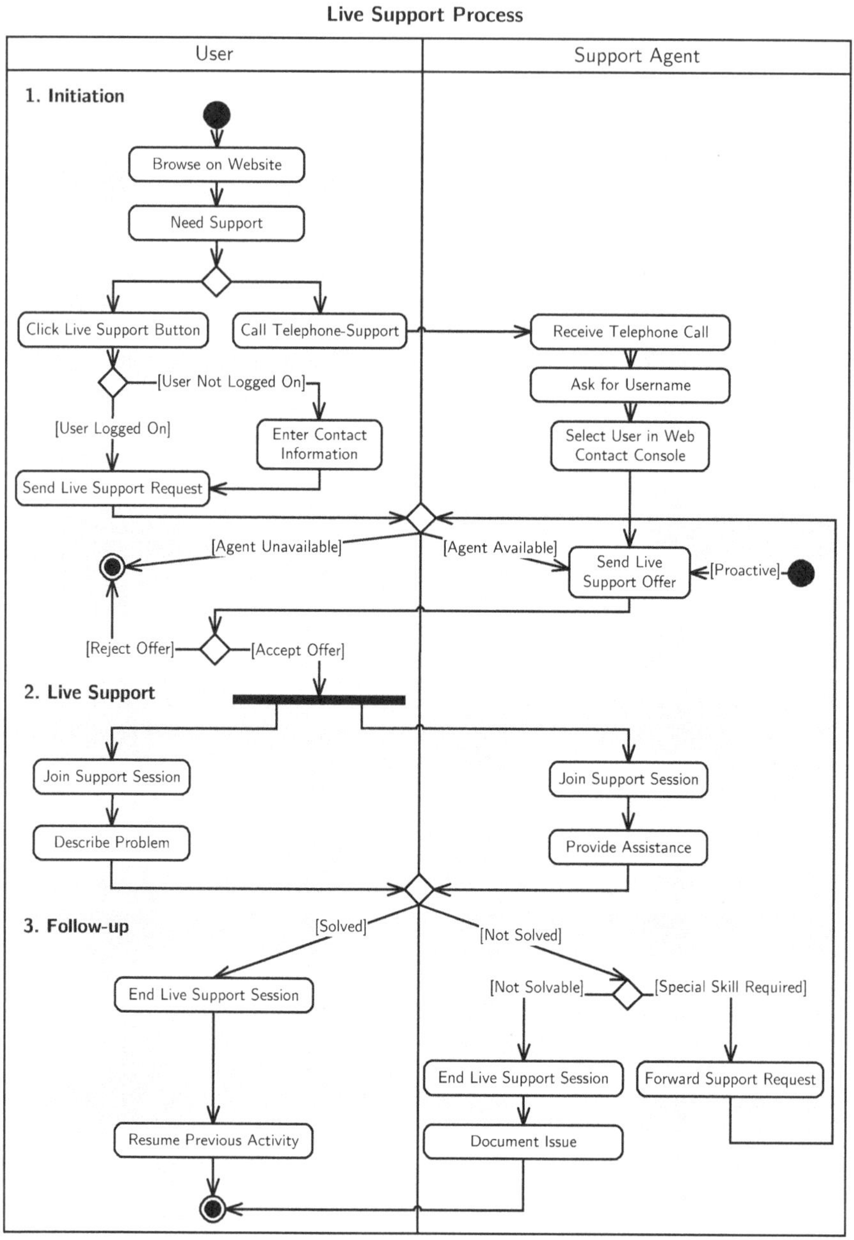

Figure 3-9: Flow of a Live Support Session

It offers functions to monitor Web users and interact with them. Agents can also choose to proactively initiate collaborative browsing sessions with Web users. This is particularly useful when the live support system is integrated in an online shop and customers seem to be stuck at a certain step in the order process. In any case it is crucial, that the session state of the advice-seeking user is transferred to the collaboration service. The session state includes URL of the website visited and the data currently entered in web forms (see section 3.6.4). This allows all participants to share the same view and enables support agents to provide quicker assistance and fast responses. If contact between the participants cannot be established ad hoc, it is possible to schedule a meeting and send an authenticated co-browsing invitation link via email. After initiating the meeting, the synchronous collaboration phase commences. In case of the live support scenario, this stage constitutes the actual service delivery. The user describes the problem and the support agent provides assistance in real-time.

All participants see the same part of the website and can collaborative fill in web forms. All user input is synchronized and visible. By using the awareness features the participants can highlight areas on a web page and direct the attention to them. The virtual telepointer always shows where other users are currently on a web page. Participants can be configured to have different permissions according to a customizable role concept. For instance, it may be desirable that the support agent in a live support session may only direct and guide the user, but not control the session by performing navigation actions, such as submitting web forms.

The follow-up stage ends the collaboration session. In the live support use case every participant may end the synchronous collaboration phase. In other use cases it might be desirable that only designated moderators have this capability. In case the user's problem was solved, he/she can resume the previous activity while preserving the session state modified during collaboration. If the problem was not solved there are two options on how to proceed: Either the problem is marked unsolvable and documented as an issue to be resolved later or the support request is forwarded to another support agent who has a special skill required for solving the problem at hand. Optionally, a protocol of the session and a chat transcript can be emailed to the participants.

3.10 Summary

This chapter has established the following design decisions:

- The architectural style is decentralized using a thin-server to achieve high scalability. The business logic is implemented on the client side. The server merely functions as a mediating proxy forwarding event notifications between clients.

- To control synchronization of events and collaboration related features only browser-native functionality is used. Solution approaches for overcoming the limitations of previous collaboration systems have been presented.

- To increase workspace awareness, a chat, highlight functions, and replicated mouse pointers (telepointers) are used.

- By using a locking mechanism, interferences occurring during collaborative session are avoided.

Technical feasibility of the design decision has been shown by elaborating on special solution approaches to problems that previously prevented the design of real-time collaboration using only browser-native functionality. Based on the conceptual foundations, the implementation is presented in the following chapter. Problems and challenges are highlighted in particular.

4 Implementation

This chapter presents selected implementation details based on the established solution design. It is explained how the components of the collaboration service operate and which role each one plays in synchronizing browser interactions. Given the decentralized replication approach in which the server's primary role is that of a mediator the description focuses on the client-side application logic in particular. An emphasis is put on the primary challenge of realizing the designed synchronization mechanism on the browser-native platform. As recommended by Fettke (2010), it is pointed out, what contributions the use of particular techniques involve in terms of the intended design goals (see section 3.2). Alternative strategies to achieve the design goals are described and the benefits as well as drawbacks of each technique are discussed.

4.1 System Overview

Figure 4-1 illustrates the event-driven architecture as it is used for the prototype. The figure abstracts from technical details and presents a high level view on the components employed.

The system is comprised of two major parts. The Collaboration Client is coded entirely in JavaScript and uses native cross-browser compatible functionality only. It provides all features required for monitoring and replicating user interactions and events occurring in the browser. As all client configurations such as the presenter and the viewer profiles strictly adhere to Web standards like HTTP and JavaScript, the system is also accessible from modern mobile devices including netbooks, tablets, and smartphones. Event notifications are managed by the Comet Client, the Comet Daemon, and the Event Services.

In order to send low latency event notifications from the server to clients, an event replication approach based on the Comet publish/subscribe architecture, introduced in SLIM (Thum et al. 2009) and REFLECTION (Schulze, Thum, and Klems 2010), is used. This approach has been proven to serve as a solid foundation for the implementation of lightweight real-time collaboration functionality. Client browsers subscribe to channels managed by the server-side Comet Daemon. This enables events occurring on other clients, such as mouse clicks and key presses, to be

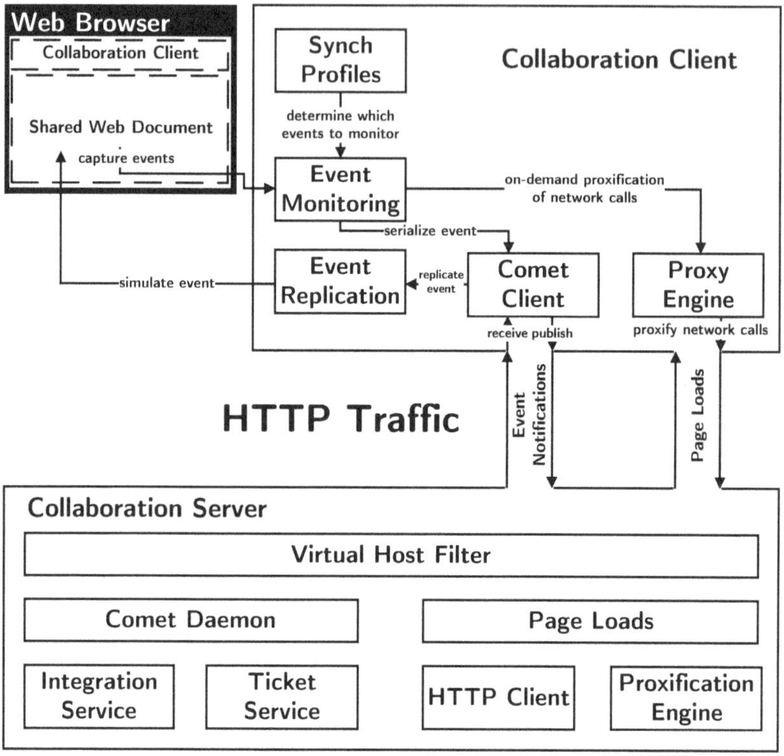

Figure 4-1: System Overview

propagated to other clients without having to explicitly poll. Thereby, scalability is improved compared to polling-based co-browsing solutions.

4.2 Choice of System Components

The following sections encompass a well-founded choice of system components, required for realizing the designed architecture. First, the solution alternatives available on the client and then the alternatives on the server-side are presented.

4.2.1 Client

To create cross-browser compatible applications, the use of a dedicated JavaScript toolkit is required. Theoretically, the use of a browser that adheres to Web standards should abstract from otherwise required adaptions to specific hard- and software environments. In practice, however, technical differences exist between browser vendors that impede Web development. As a consequence, numerous JavaScript libraries have been created. These libraries allow a structured use of JavaScript in analogy to the class and packet concept known from Java. Besides allowing clean structured code, applications can be developed relying on the advantages of object-oriented programming, such as modularity, encapsulation of data, and reuse of components (Seemann 2007). Differing from other programming languages like Java, classes do not exist in JavaScript. Instead, objects serve as prototypes whose properties can be overridden by other objects. Beyond the abstraction from browser-specific differences, providing a JavaScript Comet client that allows communication with the server-push engine is a further toolkit requirement. Taking the lead, such a client was first implemented as a part of the Dojo toolkit. Since 2008 similar implementations are provided by other libraries such as jQuery (Allen 2008) and Mootools (Hutchins 2008). For the implementation of the prototype, the Dojo toolkit is deemed best suited. The toolkit is developed by the Dojo foundation sponsored by Oracle, IBM and AOL[15].

4.2.2 Server

The server was implemented using Java EE. It acts as a mediator intercepting HTTP messages passed between the client browsers and the target host. For realizing the designed real-time communication layer functionality, a Web container supporting asynchronous non-blocking input/output operations is required. This is an important prerequisite to scalable client-to-client event propagation (see section 3.5). Several frameworks which allow realizing server-initiated communication functionality have recently come to prominence. Atmosphere[16] and the Cometd[17] framework are implemented in Java and portable across Web containers. For the implementation, a Jetty Server is used as it also offers support for the upcoming WebSocket standard and thus provides best performance on modern browsers.

15 `http://www.dojotoolkit.org`

16 `http://atmosphere.java.net`

17 `http://cometd.org`

4.3 Web Service-based Content Adaption

As stated in section 3.4.2, the robustness of the collaboration proxy depends on the usage of a reliable Web content modification technique. So far, various modification techniques have been introduced in academic research. Chong and Sakauchi (2000) present a method for dynamic content transformation at the HTTP request/response level which allows the interception of clickable hyperlinks. Hsieh et al. (2006) use URL rewriting as a server-side technique to embed session state in Web documents. Most existing approaches require the server to parse all tags in an HTML document, which can be a bottle neck. Recently, Mao and Herley (2010) have presented a fast algorithm for identifying and rewriting links. They ignore the complex structure of HTML documents and conduct a text-based search for domain names. Their performance results show a significant improvement in performance compared to approaches that execute a full parse. However, they also point out several limitations with regard to scripted documents, hence the difficulty of link rewriting still persists. Industry examples in the area of anonymous browsing include commercial implementations such as CGI-Proxy[18] and open source alternatives such as Glype[19] and PHPProxy[20]. Similar Web service-based proxies are also used by Web usability testing frameworks such as Windmill[21] and SeleniumHQ[22]. Existing industry implementations use server-side parsers to find and rewrite URLs and thereby modify Web resources before delivery to the clients.

4.3.1 URL Rewriting Techniques

As illustrated above, it is crucial to design a robust technique for rewriting URLs. Ideally, the rewriting technique should cause minimal resource consumption on the server and avoid the need for both firewall and browser configuration. In order be able to judge the adequacy of distinct approaches it is necessary to understand the most common types of URLs encountered in Web documents. These types of URLs are listed in Table 4-1 and discussed in the following subsections.

18 http://www.jmarshall.com/tools/cgiproxy/

19 http://www.glype.com

20 http://sourceforge.net/projects/phpproxy/

21 http://www.getwindmill.com

22 http://seleniumhq.org

Absolute URLs

A1	`http://www.example.com`
A2	`http://www.example.com/path/`
A3	`http://www.example.com/path/file.html`
A4	`http://www.example.com/path/file.html?param1=value`

Relative URLs

R1	`//www.example.com`	relative to protocol
R2	`/file.html`	relative to root path
R3	`file.html` `./file.html` `../file.html`	relative to current path
R4	`#anchor`	relative to current document

Table 4-1: Types of URLs

Rewriting by Parameter. An intuitive, first attempt is to simply rewrite the URL as a parameter of a request passed to the collaboration proxy. The URL `http://www.example.com` would be rerouted as follows:

`http://proxy.com/?url=http://www.example.com`

The mediating proxy server would receive the request and construct a new HTTP traffic request using the parameter specified. While feasible for simple websites, this approach is flawed: To ensure subsequent requests are rerouted to the proxy all absolute URLs (A1–A4) and the relative URLs (R1–R3) need to be rewritten. In addition, relative URLs occurring in the document must be rewritten to absolute URLs. For instance, R3 would always be resolved against the proxy's root path. This also has the side-effect of changing the path information, which is required for the browser to return the correct set of cookies to the server. The only option to enable cookies is for the server to set the `path` property of all cookies to the root value ("/"), which causes the browser to send cookies for the URLs requested. This can of course be troublesome when the same cookie is set with different values for different paths on the same domain.

Additionally, all cookies originally intended for different domains have to be set for the proxy domain. This can cause privacy and security concerns, as cookies are accessible across domains. To minimize security risks cookies could be encrypted or encapsulated by the proxy before being sent to the client as suggested by Schreiber et al. (2010) in US Patent US 2010/0064234. However, this seems cumbersome. Avoiding rather than resolving security issues is deemed more appropriate. Hence, it is desirable to design a rewriting technique that completely eliminates these issues.

Rewriting by Path. Another approach, which preserves the ability to correctly assign cookies to requests, is to encode the information of the original request in the path of the rerouted request:

`http://proxy.com/http/www.example.com/`

To ensure subsequent requests are rerouted to the proxy all absolute URLs (A1 – A4) need to be rewritten. From the set of relative URLs only R1 and R2 require modifications. If the URL R3 was contained in a document delivered by the proxy server, it would correctly resolve against the already rewritten document URL. In contrast to the rewriting by parameter technique, cookie handling stays functional. The server simply needs to update the cookie path information by prepending the original protocol and hostname separated by a slash.

Rewriting by Hostname. Rewriting by hostname is achieved by using a wildcard entry for the proxy's domain name. The DNS server then resolves any request sent to an arbitrary subdomain to the proxy server. The example given requires the following DNS entries:

```
A        proxy.com      123.123.123.123
A      *.proxy.com      123.123.123.123
```

This limits the rewrite operation to the domain portion of the URL:

`http://www.example.com.proxy.com/`

Still, all absolute URLs would need to be adapted, but with respect to the relative URLs only R1 needs to be rewritten. R2–R4 are automatically correctly resolved by the browser. Cookie handling stays completely functional for standard cases. Only when the domain property of the cookie is set explicitly, it needs to be adjusted by appending the hostname of the proxy server. Although rewriting URLs by hostname needs an additional one-time DNS configuration, it is apparently the most efficient URL rewriting strategy. By eliminating the need to adapt most relative URLs, the number of URLs that need to be rewritten is minimized.

Unfortunately, test cases conducted have shown that inconsistent browser behavior complicates the use of this technique when using SSL encrypted traffic. Not all browsers allow a wildcard SSL certificate `*.proxy.com` to match an unlimited number of subdomains. In fact, according to RFC 2818, dealing with wildcard certificates is browser specific. More precisely, Firefox and Opera allow matching multiple subdomains. In contrast, Safari and Internet Explorer reject the certificate when more than one subdomain is used. In this case they issue a security warning. Although the collaboration service remains completely functional after users have accepted the warning, it is unacceptable with regard to the design goals. The problem pertaining to wildcard SSL not matching multiple subdomains is also noticed by Mao and Herley (2010). They suggest buying a separate certificate for each domain to be reached. This is expensive and not feasible when the number of domains browsed in a collaborative session is unknown. To overcome these issues, the dots separating the fields of the domain name of the original host are encoded as a double dashes when SSL traffic is detected:

```
https://www--example--com.proxy.com
```

Reducing the rewritten domain name to appear as a single field preserves the benefits of the rewriting by hostname technique and eliminates certificate warnings in all browsers.

Discussion. All major browsers enforce a two-connection-per-domain limit for each domain (Crane and McCarthy 2008, p. 61). Websites must not issue more than two simultaneous requests to a server. As this negatively impacts the responsiveness of many modern Web applications that make extensive use of AJAX, Web developers distribute content to multiple domains. This allows for optimized page load times. Browsers can issue more simultaneous requests leading to faster retrieval of resources. Rewriting URLs by parameter or by path disables the intended performance optimization. All requests would be issued to the same domain (`proxy.com` in the example above). Only rewriting by hostname preserves the intended optimization.

For the implementation of the collaboration service both rewriting URLs by path and by hostname are implemented. Rewriting by path is used as a fallback mechanism in cases where the proxy domain cannot be configured with a wildcard DNS entry.

Static	Anchor Tag	<a href="http://www.example.com">Static Link</a>
	Image Tag	<img src="/images/img1.png" alt="Image 1"></img>

Dynamic	Location	window.location="http://www.example.com";
	XMLHttpRequest	xhr.open("GET", document.location + "/path");
	DOM Change	document.getElementById("link1").href=url;
	Event Handler	<a href="#" onclick="window.location.replace(globalVar); return false;"></a>

[...] = URLs that need to be proxified

Figure 4-2: Identifying Static and Dynamic URLs

4.3.2 Dynamic Content Adaption

A URL in an HTML document can be statically hard-coded or dynamically created by the JavaScript engine. Figure 4-2 illustrates different uses of URLs found in Web documents. Static URLs can be found easily as they are readable before execution time as attributes of HTML tags. With the increasing interactivity of Web 2.0 applications, the number of dynamically triggered requests and hence dynamically generated URLs is increasing. Since JavaScript is a flexible object-oriented language, identifying dynamic requests is a very hard task to achieve using text-based parsing only. Mao and Herley (2010) point out "*[...] the difficulty of link rewriting mainly stems from the difficulty of finding all links contained in the document.*" Using naïve search and replace functionality over the entire Web resource often corrupts its content—some websites even become entirely non-functional when loaded. Hence, a more robust technique is desirable.

Glype and PHPProxy use a promising, hybrid approach to adapting web content. Static links found in HTML tags are rewritten using fast search and replace regular expressions. Dynamic page requests triggered by the JavaScript engine are adapted in a three-step procedure: First, a textual search is used to identify certain function or property names that are known to trigger page requests (e.g., `open`, `location`). In a second step, only surrounding code is parsed to identify function arguments and property assignments. Third, they are wrapped in a custom JavaScript function that returns a rewritten URL. For instance, the `XMLHttpRequest` listed in Figure 4-2 would be adapted as follows:

```
xhr.open("GET", rewrite(document.location + "/path"));
```

The rewrite function injected by the proxy automatically redirects dynamic links at execution time. Although this method is applicable in many cases, it might wrongly identify functions, modify parameters and thereby corrupt code. Considering a custom JavaScript object with a self-defined open method, the server-side parser would still inject the rewrite method and rewrite the second parameter, resulting in a corrupt method invocation. To avoid this problem a server-side JavaScript engine such as Rhino[23] or SpiderMonkey[24] could be leveraged to safely identify object types that potentially trigger page loads. However, as JavaScript supports prototype objects, first-class functions, fully parsing and executing the code is complex (Jensen, Møller, and Thiemann 2009). Whilst technically feasible, the overhead would limit the scalability of the server.

As a solution, synchronite implements the following strategy: Instead of wrapping the arguments only, the whole JavaScript statement is parsed and modified as follows:

```
rewriteMethod(xhr, "open", "GET", document.location+"/path");
```

The `rewriteMethod` function can now easily verify the object type of `xhr` during execution time on the client. In case it is an `XMLHttpRequest`, the second parameter of the original JavaScript statement is expected to be a URL and should be rewritten. If however the type of the `xhr` object is not recognized correctly, the original method should be executed without modification. This simple example illustrates the advantage of dynamically redirecting page requests on the client side. Although more robust, this strategy requires additional parsing effort on the server.

4.3.3 Client-side JavaScript Parsing

In line with the design goals, it is desirable to make the collaboration proxy more scalable. This is mainly achieved by taking load off the server and moving it to the clients. Keeping this in mind, the content adaption approaches can be further optimized by shifting JavaScript parsing to the client:

To achieve this goal, a trick is applied that makes use of how the browser deals with script tags. When the browser parses HTML documents and encounters a script tag, it first checks the type attribute of

23 `http://www.mozilla.org/rhino/`

24 `http://www.mozilla.org/js/spidermonkey/`

the tag. If the type is known or omitted, it loads the script's content and executes it. However, if the type is unknown the content is not loaded nor executed. Consequently, modifying the script type attribute to a value unknown to the browser prevents the execution of the scripts parsed by the browser. This permits a client-side approach to parsing JavaScript. As the browser's own script loading mechanism is purposely bypassed, a new loading engine has to be programmed that dynamically adapts the content for synchronization and subsequently executes the script. In summary, client-side parsing script has to take care of the following:

1. Retrieve the script's contents.
2. Parse the script and inject rewrite functions where page requests are expected.
3. Evaluate the script in the scope of the global scope document currently parsed.

For the correct execution of JavaScript, care has to be taken that the script tags are executed in the same order and in the same scope as in the unmodified case. To achieve this goal, the server has to append a special script tag that triggers the content adaption engine and parsing function immediately after each script tag. When retrieving the script from the server, the client has to use a synchronous blocking request.

Selective Rewriting. When bypassing the same-origin policy rather than granting anonymous access is the primary goal, it is not always required to implement a full proxy that intercepts all traffic (Hong et al. 2001). In fact, static content such as images or bandwidth-consuming video streams can be loaded directly from the remote host. For relative URLs, this is achieved by inserting or updating the `<base>` tag in the head of an HTML document. The `href` attribute of the tag points to the document base, a location against which to resolve all relative links. To decide whether to rewrite absolute URLs, the rewrite engine has to guess the mime-type of the content. For instance a URL ending with `.png` would be assumed to be an image and be excluded from URL rewriting.

4.3.4 Preserving Sessions

Being able to maintain the session state across multiple transactions is an important feature of HTTP. In a stateful Web session the content of the Web browser is not only identified by the URL of the website, but by additional state information. In an e-commerce application, the session might identify customers and include information regarding type and quantity of goods currently in the shopping basket.

In the Web domain, this state is usually encoded in browser cookies. Cookies comprise information in the form of name and value pairs that are saved by the browser. The session state can be stored in two major ways:

1. By using a so-called Session Id thereby associating the user with state information stored on the server-side or

2. by serializing the complete state in the client-side cookie.

When setting cookies, the server can declare attributes that specify how long the cookie is stored by the browser, whether it will be only sent via a secure connection, and whether it will be readable by client-side scripts. Most importantly, the domain and path attributes advise the browser for which requests to include the cookies.

In order not to break the website's functionality, it is crucial that the browser sends the appropriate set of cookies for each request even though it is routed via the collaboration proxy. This can be achieved by rewriting the cookie path and domain attributes before passing the response from the destination server to the clients. The attributes of the cookie have to be adjusted in accordance with the rewrite method employed (see section 4.3.1).

4.3.5 Caching

As not all HTTP requests are idempotent, care has to be taken in order not to re-request Web resources loaded by one client. Re-submitting a request might trigger unintended changes to server-side session state. Placing an item in a shopping cart or submitting the pay form in an e-commerce application is a request that should only be sent once. Because the synchronization mechanism relies on a replication of user events (e.g., mouse click on submit form), this case has to be accounted for. In order to prevent sending duplicate requests to the server, the contents of certain pages are cached; hence selected incoming requests can be answered by sending a copy of the already cached resource.

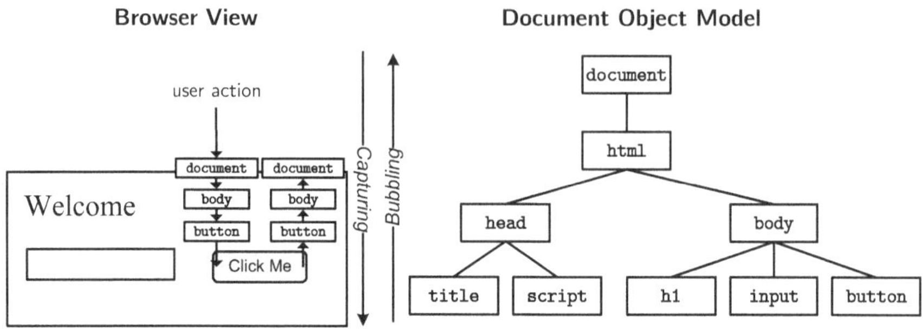

Figure 4-3: Event Order

4.4 Synchronization Strategy

This section comprises selected details of the implementation of the synchronization strategy. Solutions to the difficulties involved with monitoring and replicating events are described.

4.4.1 Event Monitoring

After the Web document is loaded in the browser, it is necessary to intercept all user events. This can be achieved by registering an event listener on the topmost node in the DOM tree. If two or more nested elements both register an event handler, the event model ensures the handlers of both elements are invoked. The execution order differs between browsers and depends on the position of the element's node in the DOM tree (see section 3.6.1). The event model is visualized in Figure 4-3. *Capturing* defines the execution order where the event travels down the DOM tree, triggering the event handler of the ancestor node first. In contrast, *Bubbling* refers to the execution order where the event travels up the DOM tree, triggering the event handler of the descendent node first. This behavior is standardized in the DOM Level 2 Events Specification (W3C 2000).

Only after the event has triggered all event listeners without being cancelled, the default action corresponding to the event is executed. A `mouseclick` event triggered on an anchor tag would, for instance, result in the browser to load the URL specified in the `href` property of the tag. Correspondingly, a click on a submit button would result in the form to be submitted to the URL specified in the `action` attribute. Once an

```
01 [{
02   channel:"/2DC345/mouseclick", clientId:"1akzbb1ztwu6xeiflai", id:"42",
03   data:{
04     cssSelector:{element:"input[name='q']", frame:"catalog"},
05     mouseEvent:{type:"click", canBubble:false, cancelable:true, screenX:1157,
06                 screenY:378,  clientX:1157, clientY:205, ctrlKey:false,
07                 altKey:false, shiftKey:false, metaKey:false, button:0}
08     userName:"John Smith",
09     nOffset:{nx:0.226775956284153, ny:0.9545454545454546}
10   }
11 }]
```

Table 4-2: Serialized User Event

event is intercepted by the collaboration client, it is processed in two steps: First, it is checked whether the default action triggered by the event needs to be adapted by rerouting network calls to the collaboration proxy. Rewriting URLs is done on-demand to achieve faster page loads times and hence a more responsive user experience.

Second, the information to recreate the event is serialized in JSON format. This event information is encapsulated as a Comet message published to other participating clients. For example, an intercepted click on a text input field is published as a JSON data structure illustrated in Table 4-2. For events that trigger multiple times a millisecond, such as `mousemove` and `scroll`, intermediate values are discarded. To improve scalability, these events are only published at pre-defined intervals. Besides the Comet meta data (2), the message is comprised of an identifier for the event target (4) as well as all information necessary to replicate the event on participating clients (5–7).

4.4.2 Event Replication

Replicating events in different browsers is a complex task. By default, it is not possible to simulate user actions in the browser. Simply executing the default action of events is not sufficient. It does not result in the same user experience and the website's functionality might be broken. For instance, it has become popular for dynamic websites to use automatic suggestions in search fields as keys are typed. The default action of the `keypress` Event is to input the character typed in the input field focused. The automatic suggestion functionality is broken when simply synchronizing the characters typed in input fields instead of replicating the event that triggers the change of the value and allows execution of embedded event handlers that might trigger additional UI changes. Such UI changes may include the display of a suggestion box that can be used for automatic text completion.

As a solution to this problem and to preserve the site's dynamic functionality, it is required to dispatch artificial events to the corresponding DOM nodes adhering to the event flow created by real user actions. In W3C compliant browsers dispatching artificial events can be achieved by using the `createEvent`, `initEvent`, and `dispatchEvent` methods. Microsoft Internet Explorer that does not adhere to the W3C standard uses a proprietary event dispatch system.

Early tests have shown that dispatching artificial events does not result in synchronizing the views in all browsers. In fact, only some artificial events in some browsers cause the default action to be executed. For example, triggering a `mouseclick` event as shown in Table 4-2 does not result in the input field to receive the focus. Handling artificial `keypress` events is also inconsistent across browsers. While in Firefox the artificial event results in the character to be typed in the input field, Internet Explorer does not execute this default behavior. This inconsistent browser behavior complicates the implementation of the event replication mechanism.

To overcome this issue, the collaboration client automatically checks the browser's capabilities by conducting feature tests in the background. The test results are used to infer how events can be reliably and robustly replicated. One test, for instance, involves inserting a text input field, dispatching a `keypress` event, and then checking whether the value of the text input field has been changed accordingly. If the value has not changed, the system infers that in addition to dispatching the event the default action has to be executed.

Using this approach rather than adapting the behavior for specific predefined browsers allows the collaboration client to learn and to be agnostic to the execution environment enabling it to better support untested environments and future browser versions.

4.5 Multi-user Awareness

One important part of the implementation is to ensure usability by providing different awareness features. All participants need to be informed about actions performed by other users in the same session. Actors need to see what other actors are doing and what part of the shared object they are viewing. Figure 4-4 shows a screenshot of an active collaboration session between Alice and Bob. The window on the bottom shows Bob as he enters text in the search field. Alice's view of the same situation is shown on the top of the figure.

4.5.1 Telepointer

To make sure the telepointer can seamlessly move across frames containing multiple documents, it is inserted as a `div` node in the topmost document. Setting the `z-index` CSS property of the node ensures visibility on all documents. To mimic the behavior of a real cursor, the icon used to display the telepointer is adjusted according to the underlying HTML node (hand, arrow, text select). A name tag, which is attached to the telepointer, identifies the remote user.

4.5.2 Annotations

As simple replication of the mouse pointer might not be sufficient to allow for gestural communication, an additional highlight and annotation functionality has been implemented. Using only CSS properties, selected nodes can be highlighted using a fading color animation. If the node clicked upon exceeds a certain size that would make highlighting meaningless or disturbing, a circular highlight animation is played instead.

4.5.3 Typing Indicator

The typing indicator is not only used in the chat window as in many existing instant messaging services. Instead, it is also attached to text `input` and `textarea` nodes. This ensures that all users know who is currently editing form fields.

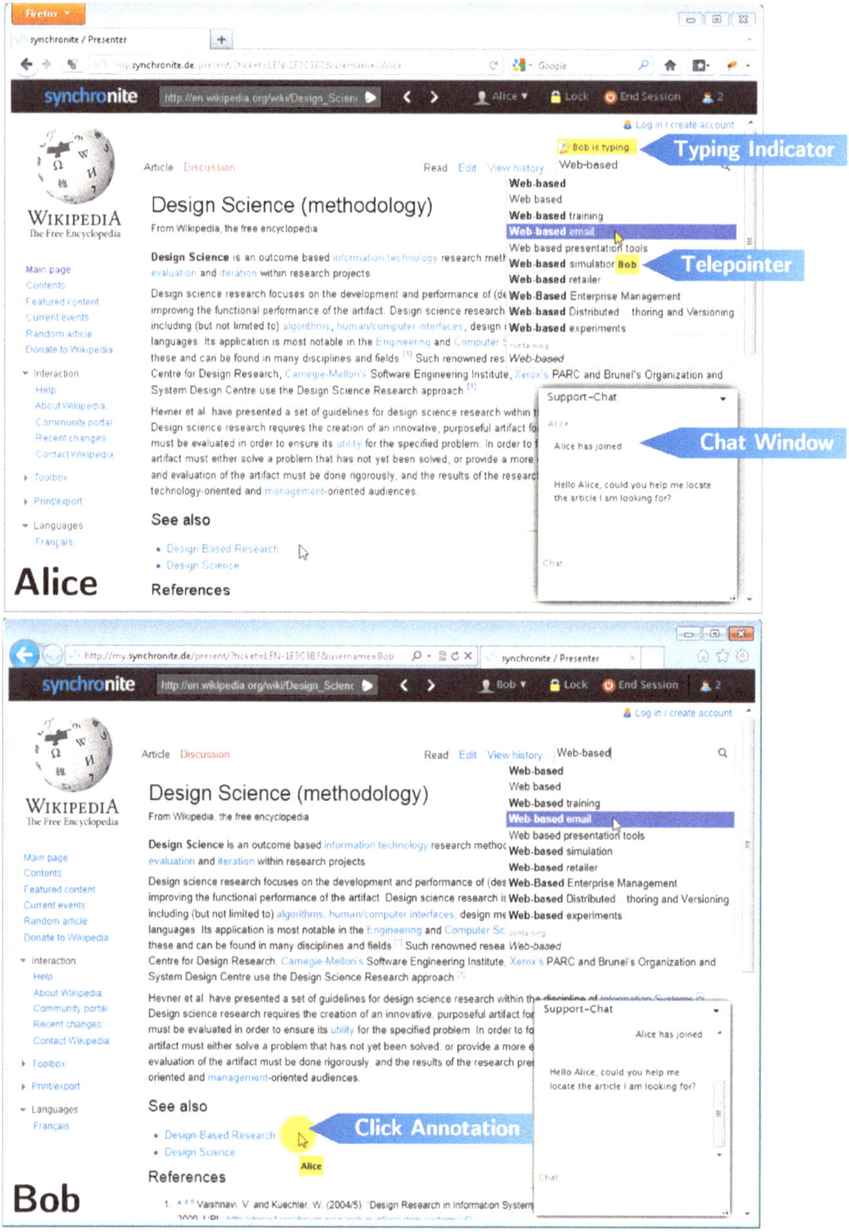

Figure 4-4: Illustration of Awareness Features

```
<html>
  <head>
    <script type="text/javascript" src="integration.js"></script>
    ...
  </head>
  ...
</html>
```

Table 4-3: Synchronous Script Loading

4.6 Integration in Third-party Websites

Placing a dynamic live support button on a webpage requires embedding JavaScript. A naïve way of integrating the collaboration service in third-party websites is directly loading a JavaScript file from an external server. This is usually done using a script tag which points to a script file through the `src` attribute as illustrated in Table 4-3.

According to the execution model followed by all Web browsers, JavaScript files are processed synchronously before the page is rendered and the `load` event is triggered. Some browsers also block resource downloads. The rationale behind this is that the browser does not know the content of the script files, before completely downloading and parsing them. Scripts may alter the DOM tree or redirect the browser to a new webpage. If this happens any further resources such as images are not required and thus do not need to be downloaded.

Testing the synchronous script loading approach showed that page loads were slower after integration. To emphasize the effect for testing purposes, the server is intentionally configured to defer the delivery of the integration script by 50 ms. As can be seen in Figure 4-5, the embedded script file blocks the rendering process and slows down the page load of Web documents. The loading speed of a webpage is illustrated by two

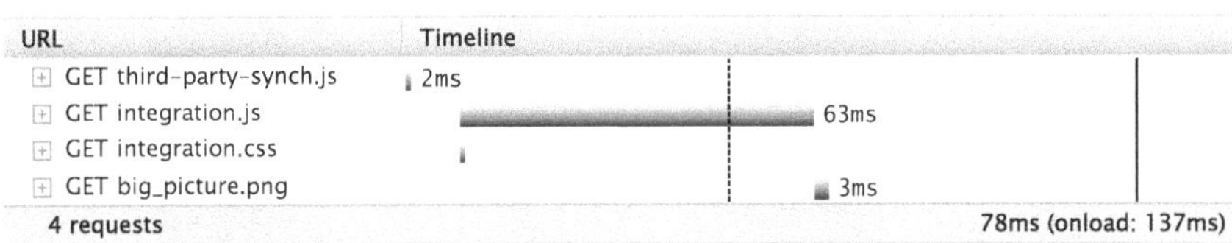

Figure 4-5: Performance Analysis of Synchronous Script Loading

```
<html>
  <head>
    <script type="text/javascript">
      (function() {
        var s = document.createElement("script");
        s.type = "text/javascript";
        s.async = true;
        s.src = window.location.protocol + "//proxy.de/integration.js";
        var st = document.getElementsByTagName('script')[0];
        st.parentNode.insertBefore(s, st);
      })();
    </script>
  </head>
  ...
</html>
```

Table 4-4: Asynchronous Script Loading

vertical lines in the graph. The dotted line marks the `DOMContentLoaded` event that triggers when the DOM of the page is ready, but related stylesheets, images, and nested frames may not have finished loading. The solid line marks the actual `load` event that fires when the browser finishes loading all content within a Web document. Because the script is loaded synchronously, the entire webpage becomes dependent on the performance of the external server that hosts the JavaScript file. If the external sever breaks the webpage may become unresponsive and stalled. In this case, the browser is waiting for a response and only resumes rendering after a timeout has occurred. In modern Web browsers, the default configuration is to timeout and idle HTTP requests after 30–115 seconds (Chuang 2007). This issue observably affects the user's experience and the overall perceived quality of the website. For these reasons, it is desirable to load JavaScript with minimal impact on the third-party website. Put more technically, it is the objective to load Java Script in a non-blocking way without delaying subsequent content from rendering. The code for loading the integration script is subject to additional requirements. It must be small to avoid extensive modifications to the third-party site and simple, so webmasters can easily include the code. Moreover, the code must be cross-browser compatible and not rely on the presence of external JavaScript toolkits, since it runs in an unknown environment. No global variables in the namespace of the third-party site must affected by the loader script.

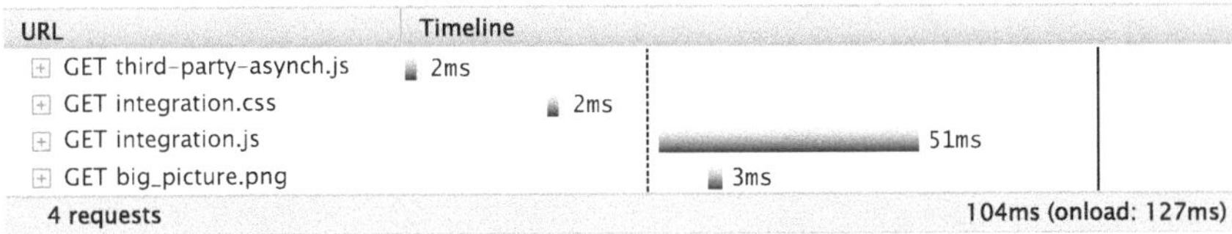

Figure 4-6: Performance Analysis of Asynchronous Script Loading

The inline script listed in Table 4-4 meets these requirements. It instructs the browser to load the integration script asynchronously in the background. This is achieved by dynamically inserting the script tag during execution time. When a script node is dynamically inserted via DOM manipulation, the default behavior is to load the code asynchronously (WHATWG 2011). A similar technique was first endorsed by Souders (2009) and is used by many SaaS applications such as Google Analytics[25].

The performance analysis depicted in Figure 4-6 shows that the script loading is still unsatisfactory. Although it is loaded asynchronously and in parallel with images, it delays the websites' `load` event (marked by the solid line) and thus slows down any startup scripts on the third-party webpage. It has to be noted that this is only an issue when the script's loading time exceeds the loading time of all original resources embedded in the webpage. To further reduce the impact of the integration script on the third-party site it is required to request it after the `load` event has occurred. To achieve this, the function in Table 4-4 is registered as a `load` event handler using DOM Level 2 functions (W3C 2000). This ensures the loader function remains unobtrusive and does not override previously registered event handlers. Figure 4-7 shows the corresponding performance analysis. It can be seen that the script is now loaded after the `load` event has occurred and therefore does not impact the performance of other scripts and resources.

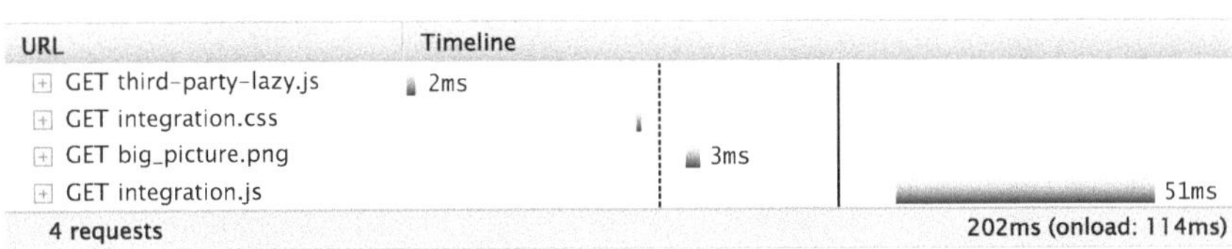

Figure 4-7: Performance Analysis of Lazy Script Loading

25 `http://www.google.com/analytics`

4.7 Summary

In this chapter, the system architecture's design was implemented using native Web technologies. In line with the design goal of minimizing the entry barriers to collaboration, only functionality of Web browsers that can be used independently of the hard- and software environment has been employed. The implementation of the lightweight real-time collaboration system constitutes a novel IT artifact as the central result of design science-based research. The artifact illustrates how Web 2.0 technologies can be used to create a generic collaboration layer supporting synchronous work at a distance. According to the guidelines published by Shaw (2003) and rules of design science by Hevner (2010), an evaluation is conducted to verify the utility of the artifact created.

5 Evaluation

The evaluation does not only take into account the technical characteristics of the proposed solution alone, but also aims to gain knowledge about its utility. In respect to this objective, Winter (2008) argues: "*What good is a highly innovative artifact the effect of which does not exceed effects of established techniques during its application?*" It is generally agreed upon that the key role of novel IT artifacts should consist of improving domain-specific information systems and work processes.

5.1 Technical Perspective

In this section, the technical properties of the newly developed solution are tested and where possible compared the state of the art. The overall goal is to gain evidence for the technical adequacy of the design decisions and the efficiency of the implementation.

5.1.1 Performance

One of the most important metrics to measure website performance is the Time To First Byte (TTFB). As the name implies, TTFB is defined as the time that elapses between dispatching a request from the client and receiving the first byte of the corresponding response from the remote host. In the following experiment the TTFB is used to quantify the latency introduced by the collaboration proxy (see section 3.4).

Experiment Setup. In a first step, the TTFB is measured for a direct request without a proxy. This allows for later quantification of the delay introduced by content adaption (see section 4.3). Secondly, the TTFB is monitored for requests that are rewritten using the different proxy techniques developed in this thesis. Lastly, the performance of existing Web service-based proxies is tested. For the test, an experimental environment is set up. It is comprised of a client accommodating a test agent and a server including several virtual machine images.

To achieve realistic results, the experiment is conducted using automated real browsers instead of load generation or Web stress test tools that try to simulate browser behavior. All requests are issued from a Windows 7 Virtual Machine running as an Amazon EC2 cloud instance. The machine connects to the Internet using 20 Mbps down- and 5 Mbps upstream. The performance measurement tool WebPagetest[26] is used to remote-control the client systems Web browser.

The different proxy solutions tested in this experiment are installed on an Ubuntu 10.04 server configured as a kernel-based virtual machine. The server is attached to the Internet on 20 Mbps down- and 10 Mbps upstream. It has 8 GB RAM, a 350 GB hard drive and a 2.6 GHz AMD Opteron processor with four cores. For the test, the system was consecutively booted using pre-configured VM-Images. Each was prepared with the latest version of the novel collaboration proxy or one of the Web service-based proxies described in section 4.3. All experiments were conducted on the same virtual host. The Wikipedia website is chosen to be the target for the request, as it uses JavaScript, CSS, and different link types as described in section 4.3.2. To reduce the effects of varying network conditions each test is repeated ten times. Before each test-run the cache was cleared on both the client and the proxy server. Although care has been taken to establish a realistic environment, it has to be noted that deployments might achieve differing results depending on special performance tweaks regarding TCP stack settings, JVM settings, and the OS choice (Bordet 2011).

Experiment Results. The average of ten test-runs for each configuration is shown in Table 5-1. In the first column, the actual time is shown in milliseconds. In the second column, the result is normalized in relation to the result for direct access. The rows are sorted in ascending order according to the overhead introduced. The complete results for all test-runs are included in Appendix 0.

The test indicates that the performance of the newly developed content adaption techniques is—in all cases—better than solutions employed by existing Web service-based proxies. The measured TTFB of the collaboration proxy is only about 24%–36% higher compared to direct access depending on the specific technique employed. One of the main reasons for this encouraging result is that most of the work load was shifted to the clients and many operations are executed on-demand, hence enabling the server to send the response faster and thereby achieve a lower TTFB.

26 `http://www.webpagetest.org`

			TTFB in ms	TTFB normalized
		Direct Access	**327.2**	**1.00**
Synchronite Content Adaption	proxy by host	selective	405.9	1.24
		full	417.4	1.28
	proxy by path	selective	426.0	1.30
		full	444.6	1.36
		Zelune 2.1	529.5	1.62
		CGIProxy 2.1beta19	593.8	1.81
		PHProxy 0.5	613.4	1.87
		Glype 1.1	804.2	2.46

Table 5-1: Test Results for Performance Measurement

Another reason lies in the efficient URL rewriting techniques (see section 4.3.1). Experiments indicate that URL rewriting by host is faster than by path. This result is to be expected as the amount of parsing effort was shown to be reduced considerably in the first case. Figure 5-1 summarizes the results and lists the proxy techniques by performance in ascending order. As discussed in section 3.4.2, the purpose of the collaboration proxy is merely to circumvent the same-origin policy rather than allowing anonymous Web access. Therefore, it is not necessary to redirect all resources contained in the responses sent by the remote host. Instead, selective rewriting techniques can be applied. This allows some requests

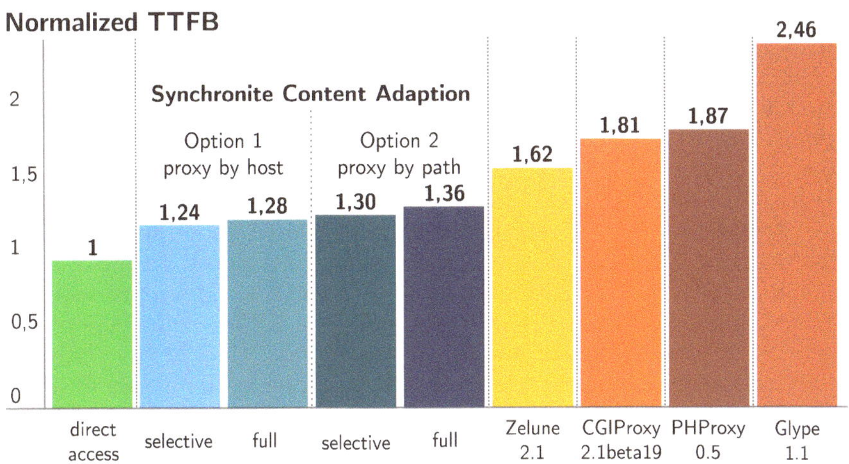

Figure 5-1: Results of Proxy Performance Evaluation

such as images and other static content to be directly loaded from the remote host. As indicated by the measurements, this accounts for an additional improvement of the server's responsiveness.

5.1.2 Bandwidth

Obviously, a reduction in network traffic can be expected as a result of transmitting events between clients rather than continuously checking for screen changes and then sending image data. The difference of bandwidth usage is calculated theoretically first and additionally tested in a practical experiment.

For example, a click on a "*scroll to top*" link can be published using a JSON data structure as illustrated in section 4.4.1. The complete HTTP request sent by the collaboration client[27] is illustrated in Table 5-2. The length of an actual JSON message highlighted in line 17 is only 433 bytes. This is about the average size of a JSON message sent by the collaboration client. To transport the message to the server, an overhead of additional 726 bytes is imposed by the HTTP protocol resulting in a total message size of 1,159 bytes ≈ 1.13 KB.

If image data was sent instead, the network traffic resulting in the same effect would be unacceptably high. Assuming the "*scroll to top*" function triggers a complete refresh of the browser's content, an image with the corresponding size of the browser's viewport, would have to be transmitted over the network. According to recent browser statistics, 85.1% of all Web users have a screen resolution higher than 1,024x768 pixels (W3C 2011). Although the entire screen area is captured, screen sharing tools use advanced delta encoding techniques to transmit only the areas changed on the screen (Ichimura and Matsushita 2005). In the example, this area corresponds to the viewport of the browser which can be assumed to be at least 80% of the screen size. Thus, an area of at least 1,024x768x0.8 ≈ 629,146 pixels has to be captured and transmitted over the network. Encoding this area with 32-bit color depth per pixel would result in 629,146x4 = 2,516,584 bytes ≈ 2.4 MB of uncompressed data. To be able to guarantee moderate quality, a JPEG compression ratio between 30:1–50:1 can be applied at maximum (King 2000). Optimistically, assuming the upper boundary, the compressed data volume would

27 The message was intercepted using wireshark, a network protocol analyzer available at: `http://www.wireshark.org`

```
POST http://proxy.de/sync/ HTTP/1.1
Host: proxy.de
User-Agent: Mozilla/5.0 (Windows; U; Windows NT 6.1; de; rv:1.9.2.17)
Gecko/20110420 Firefox/3.6.17 ( .NET CLR 3.5.30729; .NET4.0E)
Accept: text/html,application/xhtml+xml,application/xml;q=0.9,*/*;q=0.8
Accept-Language: de-de,de;q=0.8,en-us;q=0.5,en;q=0.3
Accept-Encoding: gzip,deflate
Accept-Charset: ISO-8859-1,utf-8;q=0.7,*;q=0.7
Keep-Alive: 115
Connection: keep-alive
Content-Type: application/json;charset=UTF-8
X-Requested-With: XMLHttpRequest
Referer: http://proxy.de/present/?ticket=421337&u=http://uni-mannheim.de
Cookie: JSESSIONID=1wbs7c9uxni3zw9kyuy9uiser;
BAYEUX_BROWSER=dbbf-19gks5ocvccejgor5bvum17en
Pragma: no-cache
Cache-Control: no-cache

[{
  channel:"/4213337/mouseClick",id:"29",clientId:"3fjex9qj5w6xmf7py9euo1uwhmr",
  timestamp:"Fri, 10 Jun 2011 14:12:35 GMT",
  data:{
    cssSelector:{element:"a#scrollTop"},
    mouseEvent:{type:"click", canBubble:false, cancelable:true, screenX:3452,
                screenY:419, clientX:892, clientY:248, ctrlKey:false,
                altKey:false, shiftKey:false, metaKey:false, button:false},
     userName:"John Smith",
     nOffset:{nx:0.226775956284153,ny:0.9545454545454546}
     }
}]
```

Table 5-2: Message Published by the Collaboration Client

still exceed 50,331 bytes ≈ 49 KB. This amount of data is typically sent at a rate of up to 15 frames per second until the screen is synchronized. Drawing from this small example, it becomes obvious that bandwidth compared to traditional screen sharing methods. To supplement this theoretical example with practical evidence, an experiment was conducted.

Experiment Setup. To guarantee equal conditions for each test, a Web browsing session was recorded using iMacros [28]. An integrated replay function of iMacros allows executing the pre-recorded user actions and thereby simulating the exact same browsing session several times. The automation script used to control the browser is included in Appendix 0. Executing the sequence of recorded actions takes 60 seconds and varies slightly according to network utilization. The session includes normal browsing activities, such as clicks on links, scrolling, filling out, and submitting Web forms. Before each test, the browser cache and cookies were cleared. The test was conducted using Firefox v3.6.17 on Windows 7 with a screen size of 1,600x1,200 pixels and a browser viewport of 1,597x1,077 pixels. During the experiment, the screen sharing tools tested were set to default quality.

The total upstream load was measured using Netlimiter 3[29], which allows monitoring network traffic on a per-application basis. To reduce side-effects caused by network jitter and to ensure the results are not biased, the test was repeated five times for each collaboration tool. In a first experiment, the upstream was measured only for the unsynchronized browser session in single user mode. As it is only possible to measure bandwidth consumption on a per-application basis, the only way to get to know the overhead introduced through synchronization is by calculating the difference between a synchronized browser session and a single user session.

Experiment Results. The tested collaboration tools and the results are listed in Table 5-3. Both screen sharing tools achieve similar overhead. The compression algorithm used in TeamViewer 6 seems to be better suited for synchronizing browsing session than the algorithm implemented by Adobe Connect 8. In summary, the results confirm the assumption and demonstrate that a significant reduction in network load can be achieved when employing the synchronization strategy presented in this thesis. The overhead for synchronization varies between 38% and 39%. This can be attributed to the fact, that the overhead induced by synchronization is merely comprised of serialized user events instead of graphical information for each pixel on the screen. Similar results can be achieved using other collaboration tools that rely on event synchronization only.

28 `https://addons.mozilla.org/de/firefox/addon/imacros-for-firefox/`

29 `http://www.netlimiter.com`

		Single User Session	Adobe Connect 8	TeamViewer 6	synchronite
1	total upstream[kb]	53.37	5348.45	4162.24	87.72
2		55.25	5127.48	3745.44	88.65
3		54.31	4987.28	4012.68	87.40
4		54.98	5281.17	4189.17	86.19
5		53.65	5311.08	3991.27	86.90
Ø		**54.31**	**5211.09**	**4020.16**	**87.37**

Table 5-3: Test Results for Upstream Consumption

5.1.3 Scalability

One of the design goals was to establish a scalable system for supporting lightweight real-time collaboration. In fact, much effort was made to decentralize the system and take load off the server. The objective of the following experiment is to quantify the scalability of the designed collaboration architecture by simulating a gradually increasing amount of user activity and at the same time monitoring system parameters such as responsiveness and throughput.

The responsiveness can be measured using the above mentioned TTFB metric. The throughput can be measured by the maximum number of requests processed by the server per time unit. Various performance measurements tools exist that generate load by simulating many concurrent browser requests. Because it is available for free and allows dynamic parameters in load tests, JMeter[30] is used.

Experiment Setup. As the basis for load generation, a simple collaboration scenario between User A and B was recorded: User A starts a collaboration session and navigates to the Wikipedia start page, then User B joins and receives the current session state. Both users publish a chat message, then User B clicks a link and thereby implicitly publishes a `mouseclick` event. User A receives the serialized event and replicates the click, thus requesting the same page. After recording the scenario using JMeter, a few parameter adjustments were required to make sure new sessions are created and two simulated users join one session at a

30 `http://jakarta.apache.org/jmeter/`

time. For the test 2,000 users within a ramp-up period of 60 seconds were simulated. This resulted in 1,000 parallel sessions at a time. To allow for the generation of that many requests, the load generator was placed in the same LAN. As a result, the TTFB is considerably less than in the performance test, where the emphasis was put on creating a realistic environment.

Experiment Results. In the first test, the load generation system initially only equipped with 2 GB of RAM ran out of memory resulting in the load generator to crash. The entire memory had been exhausted by creating threads that simulate users. This indicates that it was easier for the server to service the requests than for the client to simulate the load. A second test was completed successfully. The average throughput was measured to be 2.274 requests per minute and did not decrease during the experiment. The average TTFB was 29 ms. The CPU load on the server varied from 5% up to 50% and memory consumption increased from 280 MB to 600 MB. Taking into account the high number of requests, this is still a very small increase. Although the experiment was a contrived test with minimal network latency involved, it is encouraging as it underpins the lightweight character of the server.

5.1.4 Integration in Third-party Websites

To test the integration into third-party websites, it is required to alter webpages by inserting a script tag into the head section of the HTML document. This usually requires having access to the server that delivers the document. As this would limit the ability to test the collaboration functionality on real-world websites, a technique has to be found that allows injecting scripts into a Web document before it is loaded by the browser.

So-called userscripts, supported by many browsers, are ideal to be used for this purpose. Typically they allow modifying the behavior and appearance of Web documents. Currently, only Chrome and Opera natively support the installation of userscripts. Firefox and Internet Explorer require the use of plug-ins. Greasemonkey[31] is a plug-in used for enabling userscripts in Firefox. For Internet Explorer an extension called Trixie[32] is used instead. Userscripts are usually configured to be loaded

31 `http://www.greasespot.net/`

32 `http://www.bhelpuri.net/Trixie/`

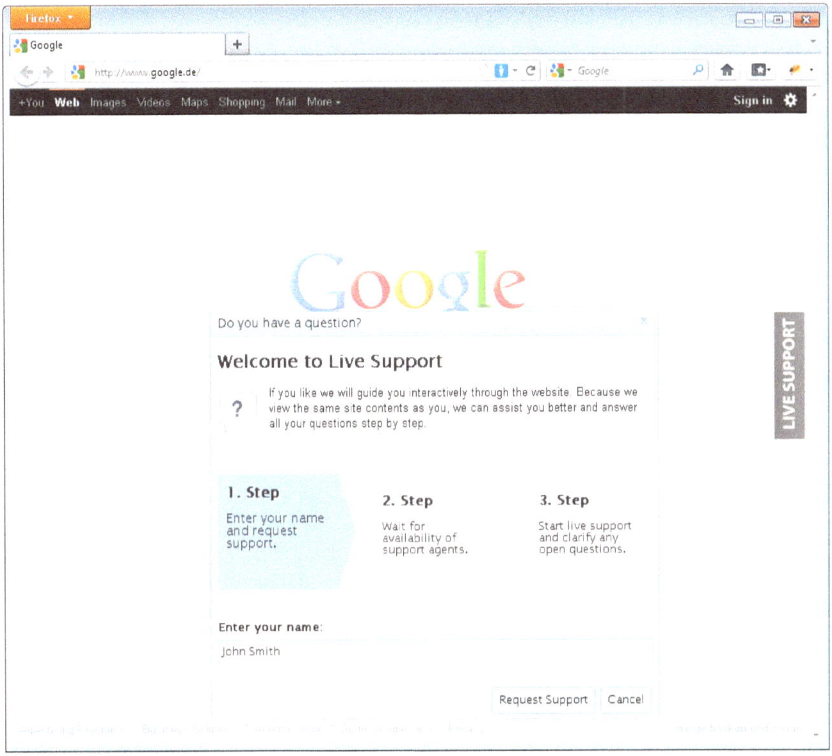

Figure 5-2: Live Support Integration Test

only for a defined set of websites. The functionality of the designed integration script is tested using the simple userscript listed in Appendix 0. This allows emulating an integration of the session handover functionality (see section 3.6.4) in real-world websites. For testing purposes, the script was successfully integrated in the twenty most popular German websites [33]. No difficulties were encountered and a support session could be established in all cases. Exemplarily, Figure 5-2 shows the integration of the live support button on the Google homepage. The figure shows the state where the test user clicked on the live support button and is asked to enter his/her name before a support agent is contacted.

33 http://www.alexa.com/topsites/countries/DE

5.1.5 Support for Mobile Devices

With increasing adoption of smartphones and modern tablets, device-specific support is an issue for many mobile applications. Typical constraints of mobile devices are small screens, low processing speed, touch interfaces, and limited bandwidth. These factors need to be accounted for when porting applications from desktop computers to mobile devices.

As the collaboration service operates transparently and merely synchronizes existing web content, no special considerations need to be made. Rather designers or developers of the website or application that is collaboratively browsed need to ensure that users get an adequate experience suitable to the capabilities of the device used. For the collaboration browsing service itself, there are no specific additional measures that need to be taken. It only requires a web browser and an internet connection and therefore is agnostic of the device in use.

Figure 5-3 illustrates the use of the same page in a collaboration session on both a desktop PC and a mobile device. Although user input is given via a touch interface on the mobile device, the event synchronization mechanism does not need to implement any functionality specific to mobile devices: When the user taps on the surface of screen, the browser on the mobile device ensures that a touch gesture correctly triggers a `mouseclick` event. This event can then be processed and replicated to other browsers in the same session (see 2). Similarly mouse movements on the desktop computer are correctly synchronized and visible on the mobile device (see 1, 3). Moreover, the webpage is automatically scaled to fit the screen by the respective browsers, so each user gets the best experience with regard to the capabilities of his/her device.

5.1.6 Summary

It has been shown that it is technically feasible to implement a collaboration proxy with minimum state information and usage requirements. As all state information is kept distributed on the client browsers, memory consumption could be reduced. This also is beneficial from a security perspective as remote cookies are only passed through the server for the duration of the request, but not stored permanently. In summary, the collaboration service incorporates efficient ways of realizing low latency collaboration and reducing data traffic at the same time.

Figure 5-3: Collaboration Service Running on a Mobile Device

5.2 Empirical Perspective

In addition to the technical evaluation it is necessary to evaluate the utility of the proposed solution by investigating its performance in practice. In academic literature the effect of IT artifacts is often measured using artificially created scenarios or laboratory experiments. Because the results observed in highly controlled environments may diverge from those produced in real world situations, the validity of such experiments is often criticized (Birnbaum 2000, p. 94). Another issue that may undermine the validity of experiments is the selection bias that may occur when test subjects are not chosen randomly (e.g., often colleagues or students are asked to participate).

In order to avoid these issues, the effect of the new solution approach is tested in a real-world live support scenario. A survey relying on proven models for quantifying service quality is conducted to find out if the novel artifact is perceived as a useful means of providing instruction and hands-on experience. How do advice-seeking users perceive helpdesk services provided via real-time collaboration? How do support agents evaluate the added collaboration capabilities? The study explores these questions by interviewing both support agents and users. Additionally, respondents are asked to compare the real-time collaboration support (live support) to other support helpdesk experiences.

5.2.1 Setup and Context of the Study

To test the utility of the solution in a live support scenario, it is deployed to the central campus management information system at the University of Mannheim. A study is conducted and users are asked to give information on their perceived service quality. The purpose of this study is to explore whether live support via real-time co-browsing is appreciated and enhances helpdesk services. Data is gathered from both users and support agents, to gain knowledge about the perceived usefulness of live support via real-time collaboration. Traditionally, a telephone helpline has been used as a means of supporting stakeholders of the campus information system (see case study in section 3.1). Both academic staff and students can consult support agents about a problem or question they have. Agents then provide step-by-step instructions tailored to the specific needs of the requester. In addition to telephone support, users are provided with online manuals and contact forms.

For the study, support agents were shown how to assist users via the real-time collaboration functionality rather than by telephone only. The live support system is embedded into the campus information system, to enhance the support services. When users contact the helpdesk via telephone, agents can decide to use the collaboration functionality in order to guide and educate users.

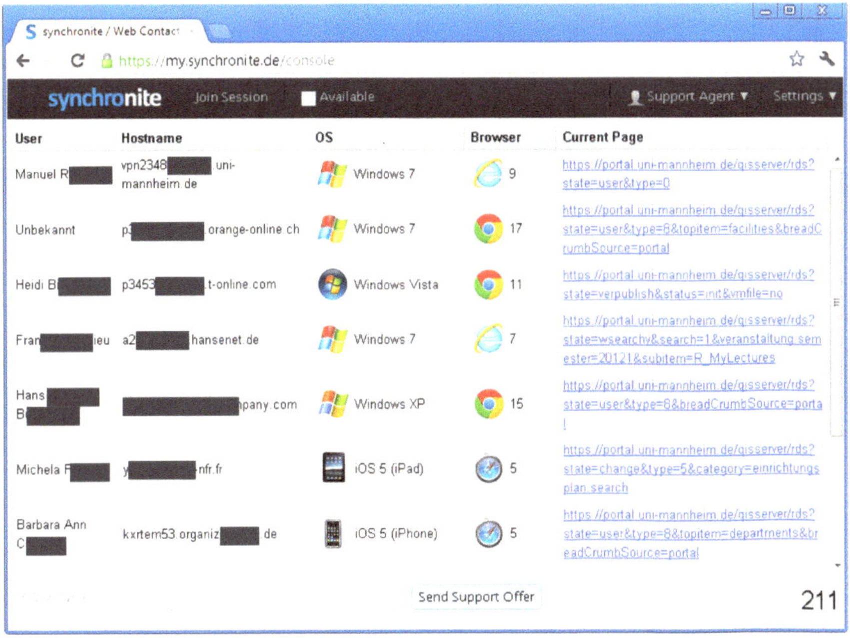

Figure 5-4: Web Contact Console for Support Agents

Establishing a live support session follows the process described in section 3.9 and is realized via two interacting components: The web contact console and the integration script. The web contact console shown in Figure 5-4 is the central point of service for support agents. It provides several functions for monitoring web visitors in real-time and establishing contact with selected users.

The grid shown in in Figure 5-4 lists all users currently browsing in the web portal of the campus information system and provides the support agent with information regarding each user. The data is retrieved by the integration script that is embedded in the portal (see section 4.6). It gathers not only personal information, such as the name and role of logged-on users, but also typical web analytics data including the hostname, operating system, Web browser, and the currently viewed page. Support agents can select a user from the grid and send a support offer. This feature is especially valuable when the user is already on the telephone line and the need to visualize instructions arises spontaneously. Alternatively, support agents can choose to be available for support requests triggered by users. When at least one support agent is available,

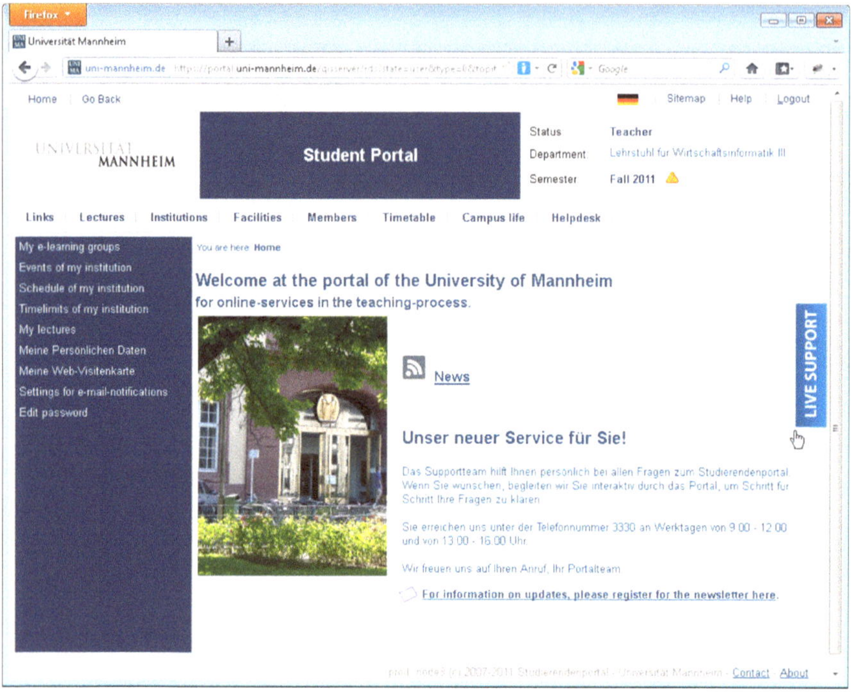

Figure 5-5: Live Support Button in Campus Information System

a live support button is displayed in the web portal as shown in Figure 5-5. Clicking the button starts the initiation stage of the live support process (see section 3.9).

After each support session, both users and support agents are prompted to complete an online survey. Data is collected using two different questionnaires. The following section discusses existing models for measuring service quality and elaborates the design of the questionnaires.

5.2.2 Design of the Research Instrument

A fundamental and crucial issue with regard to the evaluation is selecting appropriate dimensions that measure the users' perception of the support service. Few frameworks exist that can be leveraged to measure user satisfaction with support services. The popular SERVQUAL dimensions of service quality (Parasuraman, Zeithaml, and Berry 1988), which are applied in a wide range of scenarios, have been shown to be non-applicable in this context. Several studies have presented adjusted models that are better suited to measure helpdesk quality. These models serve as a basis for the design of the research instrument.

Brady and Cronin (2001) conceptualize perceived service quality based on a hierarchical approach. They build upon the SERVQUAL dimensions and a less known model proposed by Grönroos (1984). Whereas SERVQUAL quantifies service quality in terms of reliability, responsiveness, empathy, assurances, and tangibles, Grönroos measures service quality as consisting of functional and technical quality. Functional quality determines how the service is delivered (i.e., it defines the "*customers' perceptions of the interactions that take place during service delivery*"). Technical quality represents the outcome of the service act; more specifically, "what the customer receives in the service encounter." Brady and Cronin state that Service Quality can be measured in terms of Outcome Quality (Waiting Time, Tangibles, Valence), Interaction Quality (Attitude, Behavior, Expertise), and Physical Environment (Ambient Conditions, Design, Social Factors). The authors present a complete list of survey items that can be used to measure each of the aforementioned dimensions on a seven-point Likert scale (1 = "*strongly disagree*", 7 = "*strongly agree*"). The authors stress that modifications are required to account for "*industry-specific*" factors.

Such modifications have been presented by van Velsen et al. (2007) who propose adjusted dimensions for measuring helpline quality: Solution Quality and Experience of the Consultation. As the support service measured is received electronically, the Physical Environment as described in the third dimension by Brady and Conin is omitted. Solution Quality describes the correctness of the solutions offered and the promptness with which they were delivered. Experience of the Consultation reflects how customers were treated and if the service was perceived as pleasant (van Velsen et al. 2007, p. 224). Adapted items are presented and suggested for use in helpdesk or helpline scenarios. Again all questions can be asked using a seven-point Likert scale ranging from "*strongly disagree*" to "*strongly agree.*"

These items serve as the basis for the development of the questionnaire and are adjusted to the characteristics of the support scenario evaluated. Care was taken to stay close to the original constructs and not to deviate from the scope given by the corresponding dimension. Two separate questionnaires were designed, one for users and one for support agents. All questions are asked in German language.

Users. The questionnaire for users consists of seven categories and a maximum of twelve questions. To structure the questionnaire, the order of questions was aligned to the phases of the consultation process (see Figure 3-9 in section 3.9).

Table 5-4 lists the adapted items used by the research instrument. The table contains the translated items, since the original survey as attached in Appendix 0 was conducted in German. Items PD1, PD2, SD4, C3 measure the Promptness. In the previous study conducted with selected lead users, the response time was identified as an important quality criterion (cf. section 3.1.3). PD3, S1, SD1, SD2, C4 measure the Correctness. Both Promptness and Correctness impact the Solution Quality. SD3, CP1, CP2, CP3, CP4, C1, C2, C5 measure the Experience of the Consultation. Additionally, SD5 was introduced to measure whether learning could be improved by the visual instructions. OS1 measures the overall satisfaction with the consultation. AI1 was introduced to gain knowledge about the adequacy of live support for conveying additional information that while not part of the solution, is still useful for the respondent. For instance, it might be possible that the respondents get to know new portal functions and thereby improve their "*information retrieval skills*" or "*information literacy*" as a result of the guided browsing process (Graves and Desai 2006, p. 341). AI2 and AI3 collect data on technical problems that might have occurred as a result of the real-time collaboration during the consultation phase.

The questionnaires were tested on five academics and two domain experts. Minor modifications resulted from the piloting process. Some questions were worded more clearly and distinctly. It was made sure that all potential responses are captured and the overall flow of the survey was improved.

Support Agents. The questionnaire for support agents is comprised of three categories and eight questions. Similar to the questionnaire for users, the questions are ordered according to the phases of the consultation process rather than the dimensions of the underlying models. Table 5-5 contains the translated items; the corresponding online survey is attached in Appendix 0. The items PD1, SD3, C1 measure Promptness; items S1, SD1, C2 measure Correctness and PD2, SD2 measure Experience.

Question Category	Items		Possible Responses
Problem Description	PD1	It was not difficult for me to explain the problem to the agent.	seven-point Likert scale ranging from "*strongly disagree*" to "*strongly agree*"
	PD2	Explaining the problem required little time.	
	PD3	I feel the agent understood my problem.	
Solution	S1	Was your problem solved?	A1. Yes, my problem was solved during one (this) support session.
			A2. Yes, my problem was solved during multiple support sessions.
			A3. No, my problem has not been solved yet, but I was promised a solution in another support session.
			A4. No, my problem cannot be solved.
Solution Description	SD1	Did the agent propose a solution?	Yes. →Continue
			No. →Skip next item
	SD2	I have understood the proposed solution.	seven-point Likert scale
	SD3	It was easy for me to follow the steps to solve the problem.	
	SD4	Comprehending the solution required little time.	
	SD5	In the future, I am capable of solving the problem on my own.	
Consultation Process	CP1	I found the support session easy.	seven-point Likert scale
	CP2	I enjoyed the support session.	
	CP3	I found the support session hassle-free.	
	CP4	The support session was worthwhile.	
Overall Satisfaction	OS1	Overall, I am satisfied with the support.	seven-point Likert scale
Comparison	C1	In comparison to helpdesks of other organizations, the live support of the campus information system is... ...particularly user-friendly.	seven-point Likert scale
	C2	...particularly innovative.	
	C3	...particularly fast.	
	C4	...particularly good in solving my problems.	
	C5	...particularly personal.	
Additional Items	AI1	Did you get valuable information from the agent that was not directly part of solving your problem?	Yes.
			No
	AI2	Was the support session disturbed by technical problems?	Yes. →Continue
			No. →Skip next item
	AI3	What problems occurred during the support session?	(open question)

Table 5-4: Items on the Research Instrument for Users

Question Category	Items		Possible Responses
Problem Description	PD1	The description of the problem by the user required little time.	seven-point Likert scale
	PD2	It was not difficult for me to comprehend the problem described by the user.	
Solution	S1	It did not require much effort to solve the user's problem.	seven-point Likert scale
Solution Description	SD1	Did you give a solution advice to the user?	Yes. →Continue No. →Skip SD2
	SD2	I found it easy to explain the steps required for solving the problem.	seven-point Likert scale
	SD3	Explaining the solution required little time.	
Comparison	C1	I would have solved the problem faster if I had been on-site.	seven-point Likert scale
	C2	I would have found a better solution if I had been on-site.	

Table 5-5: Items on the Research Instrument for Support Agents

5.2.3 Results

The collaboration service was used 141 times during the research period. 52 questionnaires were received from users resulting in a response rate of 36.88%. Support agents returned 56 questionnaires resulting in a response rate of 39.71%. Full results are available in the Appendices 0 and I. All subsequent statistics are based on these totals.

Users. Table 5-6 summarizes the responses collected for Likert-scaled items in the user survey. Since the Likert items collected are ordinal, the median and mode are used to summarize the data in the following. The frequency of the responses is listed to express the low variability of the results. It is striking that the median is "*strongly agree*" in all cases except CP2, C4 and C5 which indicates very positive results.

The vast majority of users agree that using live support is helpful in terms of perceived Promptness. The median and mode for the corresponding items PD1, PD2, SD4, C3 is "*strongly agree*" in all cases. This is probably due to the fact that users can get connected to support agents immediately by simply clicking the live support button. Another reason may be the faster comprehension of the problem and solution as a result of shared visual context. In 75.00% of all cases the user's problem was solved in one or multiple sessions (S1). In 13.46% no feasible solution was found, and in 11.54% a solution was promised to be given in a sub-

ID	Strongly disagree 1	2	3	Neutral 4	5	6	Strongly agree 7	Median	Mean	Mode
PD1	0	0	0	0	3	16	33	7	6,58	7
PD2	0	0	1	0	5	15	31	7	6,44	7
PD3	0	0	2	1	4	8	37	7	6,48	7
SD2	0	0	0	0	0	3	32	7	6,91	7
SD3	0	0	0	0	2	10	23	7	6,61	7
SD4	0	0	1	0	1	12	21	7	6,49	7
SD5	2	1	0	2	3	5	22	7	6,03	7
CP1	0	0	0	0	4	6	42	7	6,73	7
CP2	0	1	1	6	7	17	20	6	5,88	7
CP3	0	0	0	1	8	18	25	6	6,29	7
CP4	1	0	0	1	11	10	29	7	6,21	7
OS1	0	0	0	3	5	19	24	6	6,25	7
C1	0	0	2	3	4	10	33	7	6,33	7
C2	0	1	1	3	1	15	31	7	6,33	7
C3	0	0	0	6	6	10	30	7	6,23	7
C4	0	0	1	7	6	17	21	6	5,96	7
C5	0	0	1	6	11	20	14	6	5,77	6

Table 5-6: Summary of Responses by Users (N = 52)

sequent support session. The Correctness of the solution offered (PD3, SD2, C4) was rated positive by respondents. Users strongly agree that they feel support agents understand their problem. In turn, users strongly agree that they comprehend the solution proposed by support agents. The majority of users strongly agrees that using the live support service is particularly good at solving their problems when compared to experiences made with other helpdesks.

Furthermore, the Experience of the Consultation (SD3, CP1, CP2, CP3, CP4, C1, C2, C5) was rated favorable. In particular, users strongly agree that it is easy for them to follow the advice given for solving the problem. This may be attributed to the step-by-step instructions that can be given via the collaborative browsing and joint form-filling functionality. Overall, the consultation process is rated very positive. Responses indicate that users enjoyed the support session, found it easy, hassle-free, and worthwhile. When compared to experiences with other helpdesk services, respondents strongly agree state that the novel live support system is particularly user-friendly and innovative. When asked to rate the personality of the service (C5), the acknowledgment of the user is less strong. A reason for this may lie in the fact that sending text messages via a chat is usually rated less personal than speaking on the phone or communicating face-to-face.

ID	Strongly disagree 1	2	3	Neutral 4	5	6	Strongly agree 7	Median	Mean	Mode
PD1	0	1	0	4	5	19	27	6	6.18	7
PD2	0	0	1	2	6	17	30	7	6.30	7
S1	1	2	4	2	9	20	18	6	5.64	6
SD2	0	0	0	2	7	11	25	7	6.31	7
SD3	0	0	0	3	9	15	18	6	6.10	7
C1	27	13	4	4	1	3	4	2	2.36	1
C2	33	10	3	2	1	2	5	1	2.18	1

Table 5-7: Summary of Responses by Support Agents (N = 56)

26.92% of respondents indicate that they got valuable information from the agent that was not directly part of solving the problem (AI1). Four of 52 respondents reported that the support session was disturbed by technical problems (see Appendix 0). One respondent states that "*looking on the same window was difficult [and] the system did not always work.*" The second respondent commented, that "*the transfer of commands did not work.*" In the latter case the problem was identified to be the use of an old browser, namely Internet Explorer 5.5 that does not support the modern Web technologies used in the synchronization engine. To circumvent the problem, the live support button was adjusted to be only shown when a supported modern browser is detected. Another user reported that "*the support program blocked the Web portal.*" The likely reason is again the use of an old browser version. In one case a user reported that a popup window was not shown. The reason was found to be a JavaScript function that was not accounted for in the content adaption routine (see section 4.3.2).

Support Agents. The responses collected from support agents are summarized in Table 5-7. Again, the Likert-scaled items are ordinal, so the median and mode are used in the following to summarize the data.

Responses indicate that the use of the shared visual context enabled by the live support system helped to improve the Problem Description phase (PD1, PD2). The majority of respondents agree that the description of the problem by the user required little time and it was not difficult to comprehend the problem described by the user.

Support agents state that in 80.36% of all support encounters, solution advice could be given. Results suggest that employing the live support system helped with the Solution Description. Although there seem to have been some wicked problems, respondents agree that solving the users' problems did not require much effort (S1). Moreover, respondents agree, they found it easy to explain the steps required for solving the problem (SD2) and explaining the solution required little time (SD3).

Finally, the support agents were asked to compare the live support approach to on-site support (C1, C2). In contrast to the other items, the items C1 and C2 are inverted negative Likert questions. The answers given indicate using the live support system is as good as being on-site. Support agents strongly disagree that they would have solved the problem faster or would have found a better solution if they had been on-site.

5.2.4 Summary

Overall, the survey indicates that the service quality of real-time collaboration enabled helpdesk support is perceived very positive. The median and mode of all user responses are "*agree*" (6) or better. Although the utility of the novel collaboration architecture was constantly verified with industry partners that productively used it, an empirical study was only conducted in the case described above. Consequently, the results derived for this single case empirical experiment cannot be generalized (Heinrich, Heinzl, and Riedl 2010, pp. 92–94).

6 Conclusion

Traditionally, the usage of real-time collaboration software has been mainly intra-organizational and limited to scenarios where participants agree to download and install screen sharing software. The thesis has presented an approach that removes these technical barriers to collaboration and enables *lightweight* real-time collaboration in scenarios where it has not been thought possible in the past. This was achieved by relying only on native browser functionality that is already available to every Web user. The course of the research followed a design science process consisting of problem analysis, solution design, and evaluation.

The thesis opened with an introduction of relevant concepts and technologies from the problem domain of web collaboration. Next, ad hoc use cases were outlined that have great potential of gaining benefits from real-time collaboration, but so far lack adequate tool support and hence have been unable to realize it. A thorough analysis of state-of-the-art approaches served to identify the perceived shortcomings and deficiencies of existing collaboration software with regard to supporting ad hoc collaboration. The problem analysis was supplemented with requirements elicited from a case study to ensure that besides well-established domain knowledge actual business needs are also considered.

Overall, the thesis has contributed to the knowledge base of computer-supported cooperative work and advanced the state of the art in the fields of web collaboration and software engineering. The main part of the thesis has presented the primary contribution of the research and described the architecture design and implementation of the lightweight real-time collaboration prototype. Major technical challenges that previously prevented the design of a lightweight collaboration service were identified and addressed. In line with the design science approach, the design decisions and solutions were documented comprehensively. It was shown that it is feasible to create a collaboration environment that is accessible with minimal system requirements regardless of location. Several strategies for implementing real-time notifications within the stateless HTTP protocol were presented. The design of a synchronization strategy based on the replication of user events forms a central result. Moreover, strategies for concurrency control and security features have been discussed. As opposed to existing solutions, the novel prototype allows users to engage in an ad hoc collaboration session and interact on arbitrary Web content without meeting technical requirements. The solution has been shown to run on modern mobile devices such as smartphones and tablets. Thereby, many hurdles and entry barriers to collaboration were lowered. As a secondary contribution to the knowledge base of web collaboration, a live support process model has been elaborated. Moreover, it was shown how the system can be easily integrated into existing web-based information systems.

Both applicability and utility of the novel artifact were evaluated from a technical and an empirical perspective. First, the constructed artifact was benchmarked to existing solutions with regard to performance, bandwidth consumption, and scalability. It was shown that by relying on a decentralized architecture, performance gains of 42% could be achieved. At the same time, bandwidth consumption compared to image-based screen sharing has been reduced considerably by the factor 46. The integration of the artifact in existing web-based information systems has been tested successfully. Second, the adequacy of the proposed collaboration architecture was assessed by conducting a field test in a real-world helpdesk scenario. Results of the accompanied user study have provided substantial evidence for the utility of the new solution and indicate that its usage is perceived very positive by both users and support agents. Specifically, the artifact has been demonstrated to improve domain-specific information systems and work processes. 84.84% of all advice seeking users state that using the live support service is particularly good at solving their problems when compared to experiences with traditional helpdesk channels. At the same time, support agents report that they could not have provided faster (78.57%) or better solution (82.14%) if they had been on-site.

6.1 Limitations

It has to be noted that due to the lightweight nature of the prototype it is designed to be used inside the browser's sandbox only. Although this is positive with regard to improved security and ease of deployment, it also restricts collaboration to content that is accessible from within this sandbox. While the collaboration functionality allows synchronizing Web documents that use browser extensions such as Adobe Flash or Java applets, interaction within these embedded components cannot be synchronized. Another challenge arises from malformed websites or content that does not comply with Web standards. Web browsers interpret and render such content differently resulting in diverse internal representations. Although the webpage may be displayed the same way, its internal structure is different. This has been observed to require manual configuration tweaks in the synchronization functionality. In addition, many old browsers such as Microsoft Internet Explorer 6 or other old browsers on some smartphones do not support the event transport techniques used for real-time communication. Fallback mechanisms are applied in this case; these fallbacks slow down speed of synchronization.

Finally, it is to be noted that, as Web technologies change and develop, the collaboration client and the collaboration proxy will need to be updated to comply with new standards.

6.2 Outlook

In this thesis, the proposed generic collaboration architecture was adapted to a live support scenario for evaluation purposes. The results of the empirical evaluation indicate that the novel solution helps to improve service quality. The lightweight approach allows a dynamic coupling of all parties involved in the collaboration process. The instant availability of real-time collaboration functionality may improve existing processes, particularly in situations where collective activity is occasional, spontaneous or characterized by low-frequency and short-term engagement. It stands to reason that the advanced technical capabilities need to be supplemented by new processes which facilitate structured and purposeful ad hoc collaboration. With respect to the complementary research cycle of design and behavioral science research (Hevner et al. 2004), the constructed artifact may serve as a testbed for behavioral research. New theories and models in Web collaboration can be explored and tested based on the observation and experimentation of the new solution's usage.

In the future, it is planned to adapt the generic technology for deployment in specific use cases, such as guided sales, social shopping and market research. While an increasing number of applications are ported to the Web, there is a continuous and growing demand for intense communication and coordination. In this context, the new solution presented can be a major enabler for real-time collaboration.

Appendix

A Questions for Lead Users

Personal Information

- Name
- Position, Job Role, Department
- Since when have you used the campus information system?
- How often do you use the campus information system?

General Usage of the Campus Information System and Typical Issues

- What tasks do you perform using the campus information system?
    - module catalog
    - exams
    - others
- Describe a typical issue that occurs while using the portal.
- What other issues occur when you use the portal?
    - I cannot find the information.
    - I do not understand the information.
    - The input does not generate the expected result.
    - others
- How often do problems arise?
- How do you get help when you have a problem?
    - I try to solve the problem by myself without requesting help from others.
    - I browse the self-service help pages.
    - I contact the support agents or other trained members of staff via email.
    - I contact the support agents or other trained members of staff via telephone.
- Are your problems solved?
- If no, what are the underlying reasons?
- When requesting help via email or telephone:
    - How long does it take to solve the problem?
    - What are the hurdles/barriers that occur when receiving help?
    - How can these issues be resolved? What do you suggest to improve the support process?

Integration of Live Support

Before the respondents are asked to answer the following questions, they are given a short description of the novel collaborative browsing solution.

- In your opinion, would such a solution improve the communication during the support process?
- Do you think the problems you typically encounter could be solved more efficiently?
- What features should the novel solution have to be best suited for improving the support process?
- Do you have general suggestions or advice that should be recognized before the deployment of such a solution?
- What factors are critical for the success of the deployment?

Closing Questions

- Do you have questions regarding the deployment of the tool in the campus information system?
- Do you have any final remarks?

B Questions for Support Agents

Personal Information

- Name
- Position, Job Role, Department
- Since when have you worked with the campus information system?

Typical Issues

- Describe a typical issue that occurs while using the portal.
- Are there any problems or obstacles in providing assistance and solving problems via email or telephone?
    - What kind of problems? (e.g., communication or comprehension problems)?
    - What causes the problems? (e.g., technical, organizational issues)
    - How could the problems be solved and the situation be improved?
- Is it difficult to understand the problem report given by the user?

Organization and Work Process

- How are support requests currently handled from the perspective of advice-seekers?
- Do users read the self-service help pages before contacting the helpdesk via telephone or email?
- Are there any statistics on the response time (e.g., the time needed to provide a solution)?
    - How many problem reports are submitted?
    - How many support requests are handled daily and weekly?
    - About how long does it take to solve a problem?
- How are the support requests evaluated and managed?
- Do you make use of a ticket system (such as Trac[34]) or other software that manages the support process?
- What support tools are currently in use?

---

34 Trac is an enhanced wiki and issue tracking system for software development projects available at `http://trac.edgewall.org`.

Integration of Live Support

- How would you imagine the most useful integration of a live support tool?
- What should be considered regarding the process and technical requirements?
- What features and functions should an improved collaboration tool offer to better solve the problems and support those who seek help?
- Do you have general suggestions or advice that should be recognized before the deployment of such a tool?
- What factors are critical for the successful deployment?

C Performance Results

		Direct Access	Synchronite Content Adaption Techniques: proxy by host, selective	proxy by host, full	proxy by path, selective	proxy by path, full
01	Time To First Byte (TTFB) in ms	323	454	447	457	464
02		306	398	424	421	550
03		302	403	482	410	436
04		418	417	401	418	421
05		300	407	385	447	418
06		310	406	390	460	418
07		308	389	395	470	426
08		303	393	394	387	395
09		329	410	442	402	389
10		373	382	414	388	529
Ø		**327.2**	**405.9**	**417.4**	**426.0**	**444.6**

		Zelune 2.1	CGIProxy 2.1beta19	PHProxy 0.5	Glype 1.1
01	Time To First Byte (TTFB) in ms	712	574	675	1253
02		522	598	595	750
03		500	644	578	753
04		498	512	601	753
05		509	582	591	762
06		509	631	647	760
07		515	488	655	760
08		503	667	620	745
09		492	583	587	753
10		535	659	585	753
Ø		**529.5**	**593.8**	**613.4**	**804.2**

D Browser Automation Script

iMacros-File: `recordedsession.iim`

To simulate a synchronized session, line 05 is to be replaced with a URL pointing to the collaboration proxy, e.g., `http://proxyaddress.com/?targetURL=http://en.wikipedia.org/wiki/Main_Page`

```
01 VERSION BUILD=7220523 RECORDER=FX
02 SET !REPLAYSPEED SLOW
03 TAB T=1
04 STOPWATCH ID=total
05 URL GOTO= http://en.wikipedia.org/wiki/Main_Page
06 FRAME NAME=displayContent
07 WAIT SECONDS=2
08 TAG POS=1 TYPE=DIV ATTR=ID:footer
09 WAIT SECONDS=2
10 TAG POS=1 TYPE=H5 ATTR=TXT:Toolbox
11 WAIT SECONDS=2
12 TAG POS=1 TYPE=A ATTR=TXT:Special<SP>pages
13 WAIT SECONDS=2
14 TAG POS=1 TYPE=A ATTR=TXT:Search
15 WAIT SECONDS=3
16 FRAME NAME=displayContent
17 TAG POS=1 TYPE=INPUT:TEXT ATTR=ID:searchText CONTENT=Real-time
18 WAIT SECONDS=3
19 TAG POS=1 TYPE=INPUT:SUBMIT FORM=ID:search ATTR=VALUE:Search
20 WAIT SECONDS=1
21 TAG POS=1 TYPE=SPAN ATTR=TXT:Real-time
22 WAIT SECONDS=1
23 TAG POS=1 TYPE=A ATTR=TXT:Real-time<SP>web
24 WAIT SECONDS=1
25 TAG POS=1 TYPE=DIV ATTR=ID:bodyContent
26 WAIT SECONDS=1
27 TAG POS=1 TYPE=P ATTR=TXT:The<SP>real- time<SP>web<SP>is<SP>
   fundamentally<SP>different
28 WAIT SECONDS=3
29 TAG POS=1 TYPE=SPAN ATTR=TXT:Real-time<SP>search
30 WAIT SECONDS=1
31 TAG POS=1 TYPE=SPAN ATTR=TXT:External<SP>links
```

```
WAIT SECONDS=1
TAG POS=1 TYPE=SPAN ATTR=TXT:See<SP>also
WAIT SECONDS=1
TAG POS=1 TYPE=SPAN ATTR=TXT:Difference<SP>from<SP>real-time<SP>computing
WAIT SECONDS=1
TAG POS=1 TYPE=A ATTR=TXT:real-time<SP>computing
WAIT SECONDS=1
TAG POS=1 TYPE=A ATTR=TXT:Special<SP>pages
WAIT SECONDS=1
TAG POS=1 TYPE=A ATTR=TXT:Search
WAIT SECONDS=1
TAG POS=1 TYPE=INPUT:TEXT ATTR=ID:searchText CONTENT=AJAX
WAIT SECONDS=4
TAG POS=1 TYPE=INPUT:SUBMIT FORM=ID:search ATTR=VALUE:Search
WAIT SECONDS=2
TAG POS=1 TYPE=A ATTR=TXT:Ajax<SP>(programming)
WAIT SECONDS=1
TAG POS=1 TYPE=P ATTR=TXT:Asynchronous<SP>loading<SP>of<SP>content
WAIT SECONDS=3
TAG POS=1 TYPE=P ATTR=TXT:Since<SP>then,<SP>however,<SP>there<SP>have
WAIT SECONDS=2
TAG POS=1 TYPE=LI ATTR=TXT:JavaScript<SP>to<SP>bring<SP>these<SP>technologies
WAIT SECONDS=2
TAG POS=1 TYPE=A ATTR=TXT:List<SP>of<SP>Ajax<SP>frameworks
WAIT SECONDS=2
TAG POS=1 TYPE=SPAN ATTR=TXT:JavaScript
WAIT SECONDS=1
TAG POS=1 TYPE=SPAN ATTR=TXT:References
WAIT SECONDS=1
TAG POS=1 TYPE=A ATTR=TXT:Ajax<SP>framework
STOPWATCH ID=total
```

E Userscript for Integration Test

Userscript-File: `userscript-generic.user.js`

To integrate a "*live support button*" into an existing website and enable session-handover functionality, line 07 is to be replaced with the URL of the target website.

```
01 // ==UserScript==
02 // @name                        Website Integration Test
03 // @namespace                   http://proxy.de
04 // @description                 This userscript integrates the novel live
05 //                             support module and enables session-hand-over for
06 //                             selected websites.
07 // @include                     http://www.example.com/*
08 //
09 // @version 1.0
10 //
11 // ==/UserScript==
12
13
14 // Create a JavaScript Tag
15 var proxyScript = document.createElement('script');
16
17 // Load the script using the same protocol as the target website, this
18 // is achieved using the little-known relative path "//" method.
19 proxyScript.src="//my.proxy.de/js/proxy/↩
   proxy-portal-integration.js";
20
21 // Insert in head section of the Web document.
22 document.getElementsByTagName('head')[0].appendChild(proxyScript);
```

F Online Survey for Users

Problemschilderung

Stimmen Sie folgenden Aussagen zu?

	Stimme **überhaupt nicht** zu						Stimme **voll** zu
	1	2	3	4	5	6	7
Ich konnte mein Problem dem Berater **mühelos** schildern.	○	○	○	○	○	○	○
Die Schilderung des Problems hat **wenig Zeit** benötigt.	○	○	○	○	○	○	○
Ich habe das Gefühl, der Berater hat **verstanden**, wo mein Problem liegt.	○	○	○	○	○	○	○

Lösungsfindung

Wurde Ihr Problem gelöst?

Bitte wählen Sie eine der folgenden Antworten.

○ Ja, mein Problem wurde innerhalb einer (dieser) Beratungssitzung gelöst.

○ Ja, mein Problem wurde innerhalb mehrerer Beratungssitzungen gelöst.

○ Nein, mein Problem wurde noch nicht gelöst, wobei mir eine Lösung im Rahmen einer weiteren Beratungssitzung in Aussicht gestellt wurde.

○ Nein, mein Problem kann nicht gelöst werden.

Lösungsschilderung

Hat Ihnen der Berater einen Lösungsvorschlag gemacht?

○ Ja ○ Nein

Stimmen Sie folgenden Aussagen zu?

	Stimme **überhaupt nicht** zu 1	2	3	4	5	6	Stimme **voll** zu 7
Es war **einfach** für mich, die Schritte zur Lösung des Problems dem Nutzer zu erklären.							
Die Schilderung der Problemlösung hat **wenig Zeit** benötigt.							

Beratungsprozess allgemein

Stimmen Sie folgenden Aussagen zu?

	Stimme **überhaupt nicht** zu 1	2	3	4	5	6	Stimme **voll** zu 7
Die Beratungssitzung fiel mir **leicht**.							
Die Beratungssitzung hat mir **Spaß** gemacht.							
Die Beratungssitzung war für mich **mühelos**.							
Die Beratungssitzung hat sich für mich **gelohnt**.							

Zufriedenheit

Bitte beantworten Sie folgende Frage.

	Stimme **überhaupt nicht** zu 1	2	3	4	5	6	Stimme **voll** zu 7
Insgesamt war ich mit der erfolgten Beratung **zufrieden**.							

Support des Studierendenportals allgemein

Im Vergleich zu Supportangeboten anderer Dienstleister ist der Live-Support des Studierendenportals...

	Stimme **überhaupt nicht** zu 1	2	3	4	5	6	Stimme **voll** zu 7
... besonders **nutzerfreundlich**.	○	○	○	○	○	○	○
... besonders **innovativ**.	○	○	○	○	○	○	○
... besonders **schnell**.	○	○	○	○	○	○	○
... besonders **gut** in der Lösung meiner Probleme.	○	○	○	○	○	○	○
... besonders **persönlich**.	○	○	○	○	○	○	○

Zusätzliche Informationen

Haben Sie von Ihrem Berater für Sie relevante oder wertvolle Informationen erhalten, die nichts unmittelbar mit der Lösung Ihres Problems zu tun haben?

○ Ja ○ Nein

Wurde die Beratungssitzung durch technische Probleme beeinträchtigt?

○ Ja ○ Nein

Umfrage verlassen und löschen

Absenden

G Online Survey for Support Agents

Problemschilderung

Stimmen Sie folgenden Aussagen zu?

	Stimme **überhaupt nicht** zu						Stimme **voll** zu
	1	2	3	4	5	6	7
Die Schilderung des Problems hat **wenig Zeit** benötigt.	○	○	○	○	○	○	○
Ich hatte keine Schwierigkeit zu **verstehen**, wo das Problem des Nutzers liegt.	○	○	○	○	○	○	○

Lösungsfindung und –Schilderung

Stimmen Sie folgenden Aussagen zu?

	Stimme **überhaupt nicht** zu						Stimme **voll** zu
	1	2	3	4	5	6	7
Ich hatte **keine Mühe**, das Problem des Nutzers zu lösen.	○	○	○	○	○	○	○

Haben Sie dem Nutzer einen Lösungsvorschlag gemacht?

○ Ja ○ Nein

Stimmen Sie folgenden Aussagen zu?

	Stimme **überhaupt nicht** zu						Stimme **voll** zu
	1	2	3	4	5	6	7
Es war **einfach** für mich, die Schritte zur Lösung des Problems dem Nutzer zu erklären.	○	○	○	○	○	○	○
Die Schilderung der Problemlösung hat **wenig Zeit** benötigt.	○	○	○	○	○	○	○

Vergleich zur Vor-Ort-Berartung

Stimmen Sie folgenden Aussagen zu?

	Stimme **überhaupt nicht** zu						Stimme **voll** zu
	1	2	3	4	5	6	7
Ich hätte das Problem **schneller gelöst**, wenn ich **vor Ort** gewesen wäre.	○	○	○	○	○	○	○
Ich hätte eine **bessere Lösung** für das Problem gefunden, wenn ich **vor Ort** gewesen wäre.	○	○	○	○	○	○	○

Umfrage verlassen und löschen

Absenden

H Survey Data of Users

Numbers indicate the answer given on a seven-point Likert scale ranging from 1 = "*strongly disagree*" to 7 = "*strongly agree*".

ID	PD1	PD2	PD3	S1	SD1	SD2	SD3	SD4	SD5	CP1	CP2	CP3	CP4	OS1	C1	C2	C3	C4	C5	AI1	AI2	AI3
01	6	5	5	A2	Y	6	6	5	5	6	6	6	5	6	6	7	5	6	6	Y	N	6
02	6	7	7	A1	Y	7	7	7	7	5	4	5	5	6	7	7	4	4	5	N	N	6
03	7	7	7	A1	Y	7	7	7	7	7	7	7	7	7	7	7	7	7	7	N	N	7
04	7	7	7	A1	Y	7	7	7	7	7	6	6	7	7	6	6	7	7	7	Y	N	7
05	5	6	5	A1	Y	6	5	7	7	7	6	6	5	6	6	7	6	6	7	Y	N	5
06	7	7	7	A3	N					5	5	5	5	7	4	4	4	5	6	N	Y	7
07	6	6	6	A1	N					7	7	7	5	7	6	6	6	5	5	Y	N	6
08	7	7	7	A1	Y	7	7	7	7	7	7	7	7	7	7	7	7	7	6	Y	N	7
09	6	5	3	A4	N					7	7	7	5	4	7	7	7	4	5	N	N	6
10	7	7	7	A1	Y	7	7	7	7	7	7	7	7	7	7	6	7	7	7	N	N	7
11	7	7	7	A4	Y	7	7	7	1	7	2	7	1	4	4	4	6	4	4	N	N	7
12	7	7	7	A1	Y	7	7	7	7	7	7	7	7	7	6	6	5	5	5	Y	N	7
13	7	6	7	A1	Y	7	6	6	7	7	7	7	7	7	7	7	7	7	7	N	N	7
14	7	7	7	A1	Y	7	7	7	7	7	6	7	7	7	7	6	6	6	7	N	N	7
15	7	7	7	A1	Y	7	6	7	7	7	7	7	7	7	7	7	7	7	6	N	N	7
16	7	3	7	A3	Y	7	5	3	2	7	7	5	5	6	5	4	5	5	6	N	Y	7
17	6	5	5	A4	Y	7	7	6	4	7	6	7	5	5	7	7	6	4	6	N	N	6
18	7	6	7	A1	Y	7	7	6	7	7	7	7	6	7	7	7	7	6	4	N	N	7
19	7	7	7	A3	Y	7	7	7	1	7	4	7	7	6	7	7	7	7	7	N	N	7
20	7	7	7	A1	Y	7	7	7	7	7	7	7	7	7	7	7	4	7	5	N	N	7
21	7	7	7	A1	Y	7	7	7	7	7	7	7	7	7	7	7	7	7	6	N	N	7
22	7	7	7	A1	Y	7	7	7	6	7	7	7	7	7	7	7	7	7	7	Y	N	7
23	7	7	7	A4	Y	7	7	7	4	7	4	7	7	7	5	5	7	5	5	N	N	7
24	7	6	7	A1	N					7	6	6	7	6	7	7	7	6	6	N	N	7
25	7	6	7	A1	N					7	6	6	7	7	7	7	7	6	5	N	N	7
26	5	6	3	A2	Y	7	7	6	7	7	6	6	7	6	3	3	4	4	3	N	N	5
27	7	7	7	A1	Y	7	7	6	7	7	6	7	7	7	7	7	7	7	6	Y	N	7
28	6	7	7	A1	Y	7	7	7	6	7	7	6	7	6	7	7	7	7	7	N	N	6
29	6	5	6	A1	N					5	4	6	5	5	3	2	4	4	4	Y	N	6
30	7	6	6	A1	Y	7	7	7	7	7	6	6	7	7	7	6	7	7	6	Y	N	7
31	7	7	7	A1	Y	7	6	6	5	7	6	6	7		7	6	6	6	7	N	N	7
32	7	7	7	A2	Y	7	7	6	5	6	7	7	7	7	7	7	7	7	6	Y	Y	7
33	6	6	6	A1	Y	7	7	6	7	6	4	5	7	6	7	7	7	7	5	N	N	6
34	7	7	7	A3	N					7	5	7	7	7	6	7	7	7	4	Y	N	7
35	6	7	6	A2	N					7	6	6	7	7	7	7	7	7	6	N	N	6
36	6	6	7	A1	Y	6	6	6	6	6	7	6	6	6	7	7	7	7	5	N	N	6
37	5	5	4	A4	N					6	3	4	5	6	6	6	7	3	4	N	N	5
38	7	7	7	A2	Y	7	6	6	7	7	6	7	7	6	7	6	6	6	6	N	Y	7
39	7	7	7	A3	N					7	6	6	6	5	7	6	4	6	7	N	N	7
40	6	6	7	A1	N					7	5	5	7	5	7	7	7	6	5	N	N	6
41	7	7	6	A2	Y	7	7	6	7	7	6	7	7	7	6	7	5	6	6	N	N	7
42	7	7	7	A1	Y	7	6	6	7	7	5	6	6	6	5	7	7	7	6	N	N	7
43	7	7	6	A1	N					7	6	5	6	6	7	6	7	6	7	N	N	7

44	7	6	7	A2	Y	7	7	7	6	7	7	7	6	7	7	7	5	6	6	Y	N	7
45	6	6	7	A1	Y	7	6	7	6	6	5	6	6	6	7	7	5	6	6	N	N	6
46	7	7	7	A1	N					7	7	6	6	6	6	7	7	7	7	N	N	7
47	7	6	5	A4	N					7	7	6	6	4	7	6	7	4	6	Y	N	7
48	7	7	7	A4	N					7	5	5	4	6	6	7	7	7	5	N	N	7
49	6	6	7	A3	N					7	6	6	5	5	4	6	6	6	6	N	N	6
50	6	7	7	A1	Y	7	6	7	7	5	4	5	6	6	5	6	6	5	4	N	N	6
51	6	7	6	A1	N					7	5	7	7	6	7	6	7	6	6	N	N	6
52	6	7	7	A2	Y	7	6	7	7	7	7	7	7	7	7	7	6	6	7	N	N	6

ID	Technical Problems – Original (German)
06	Blick aufs gleiche Fenster schwierig, System funktionierte nicht immer.
16	Übertragung von Kommandos nicht durchgereicht.
32	Supportprogramm hat das Portal blockiert.
38	Popupfenster wurde nicht angezeigt.

ID	Technical Problems – Translated
06	Looking at the same window was difficult [and] the system did not always work.
16	Transfer of commands did not work.
32	The support program blocked the Web portal.
38	Popup window was not shown.

I Survey Data of Support Agents

Numbers indicate the answer given on a seven-point Likert scale ranging from 1 = "*strongly disagree*" to 7 = "*strongly agree*".

ID	PD1	PD2	S1	SD1	SD2	SD3	C1	C2
01	5	6	6	Y	6	6	4	4
02	7	6	6	Y	6	5	2	1
03	6	7	7	Y	7	6	1	1
04	4	4	3	N			4	5
05	6	6	2	Y	5	4	1	1
06	5	5	5	Y	5	5	2	3
07	7	7	6	Y	6	6	2	2
08	7	7	6	Y	7	6	6	7
09	5	5	5	Y	5	5	1	1
10	2	3	3	Y	4	4	5	3
11	7	7	6	Y	7	7	1	1
12	6	7	5	N			1	1
13	7	7	6	Y	6	5	1	1
14	7	7	6	Y	7	7	1	1
15	6	5	7	Y	7	6	1	1
16	7	7	7	Y	7	7	1	1
17	7	7	7	Y	7	7	1	1
18	6	6	6	Y	6	6	6	6
19	4	4	2	N			1	1
20	6	6	5	Y	6	6	3	3
21	7	7	5	N			1	1
22	7	7	7	Y	7	7	1	1
23	7	7	7	Y	7	7	1	1
24	6	5	7	Y	6	7	2	2
25	6	7	6	Y	6	6	1	1
26	5	6	7	Y	5	6	1	1
27	7	6	5	Y	6	5	1	1
28	6	6	4	Y	5	5	2	2
29	6	6	3	N			2	2
30	4	5	1	N			1	1
31	7	7	7	Y	7	7	7	7
32	7	7	7	Y	7	7	7	7
33	7	7	6	Y	7	7	6	7
34	7	7	7	Y	7	7	7	7
35	7	7	7	Y	7	7	7	6
36	7	7	5	Y	5	5	2	2
37	6	7	6	Y	5	6	2	1
38	6	7	7	Y	7	6	2	1
39	7	6	7	Y	7	7	1	1
40	6	7	7	Y	7	7	1	1
41	7	7	7	Y	6	6	1	1
42	5	7	6	Y	7	7	2	1
43	7	6	7	Y	7	7	1	1

44	7	6	6	N			4	4
45	7	7	6	Y	7	6	3	1
46	6	7	6	N			3	2
47	6	7	7	Y	7	6	2	1
48	7	6	5	Y	7	6	1	2
49	4	5	3	Y	4	4	4	1
50	6	7	5	Y	6	5	2	1
51	6	6	4	N			1	1
52	7	6	6	N			1	1
53	6	6	6	Y	7	7	1	2
54	6	7	6	N			3	2
55	7	7	6	Y	7	7	1	1
56	7	6	6	Y	7	5	2	2

References

Allen, M. 2008. Implementation of the Bayeux Protocol for jQuery. Comet jQuery Plugins. http://plugins.jquery.com/project/Comet (Accessed: January 17, 2010).

Aoki, Y. 2002. Multimedia Communication Systems: Building a Collaborative Web Environment for Supporting End Users. IPSJ Journal Vol. 43, No. 2, pp. 530–542.

Atterer, R., A. Schmidt, and M. Wnuk. 2007. A Proxy-based Infrastructure for Web Application Sharing and Remote Collaboration on Web Pages. In: Human-Computer Interaction—INTERACT 2007, C. Baranauskas, P. Palanque, J. Abascal, and S. D. J. Barbosa (Eds.), Vol. 4662, pp. 74–87. Lecture Notes in Computer Science. Berlin, Heidelberg: Springer, ISBN 978-3-540-74794-9.

Bentley, R., T. Horstmann, and J. Trevor. 1997. The World Wide Web as Enabling Technology for CSCW: The Case of BSCW. Computer Supported Cooperative Work (CSCW) Vol. 6, No. 2, pp. 111–134.

Berners-Lee, T., R. Fielding, and H. Frystyk. 1996. HyperText Transfer Protocol—HTTP/1.0. Network Working Group RFC 1945. http://www.ics.uci.edu/pub/ietf/http/rfc1945.html (Accessed: June 24, 2010).

Birnbaum, M. H. 2000. Psychological Experiments on the Internet. London: Academic Press, ISBN 978-0-12-099980-4.

Bo, J., B. Jiajun, C. Chun, and S. Mingli. 2004. Semantic Locking in Real-time Internet-based Collaborative Graphics Design Systems. In: Proceedings of the TENCON IEEE Region 10 Conference, Vol. B, pp. 282–285.

Bordet, S. 2011. Load Testing. CometD Documentation. http://cometd.org/documentation/howtos/loadtesting (Accessed: June 17, 2011).

Brady, M. K. and J. J. Cronin. 2001. Some New Thoughts on Conceptualizing Perceived Service Quality: A Hierarchical Approach. Journal of Marketing Vol. 65, No. 3, pp. 34–49.

Bu, J., B. Jiang, J. Yang, and C. Chen. 2006. Telepointer Motion Prediction in Real-time Internet-based Collaborative Graphics Editing Systems. In: Proceedings of the 10th International Conference on Computer Supported Cooperative Work in Design (CSCWD'06), pp. 1–5.

Bughin, J. and J. Manyika. 2007. How Businesses are Using Web 2.0: A McKinsey Global Survey. McKinsey Quaterly. http://www.mckinseyquarterly.com/article_page.aspx?ar=1913 (Accessed: May 7, 2010).

BVH. 2010. Versand- und Online-Handel (B2C). In: Jahresprognose und Zwischenergebnis der Studie „Distanzhandel in Deutschland 2010" (BVH-Jahrespressekonferenz 2010).

Callegati, F., W. Cerroni, and M. Ramilli. 2009. Man-in-the-middle Attack to the HTTPS Protocol. IEEE Security & Privacy Vol. 7, No. 1, pp. 78–81.

Campbell, J. D. 2002a. Multi-user Collaborative Visual Program Development. In: IEEE 2002 Symposia on Human Centric Computing Languages and Environments (HCC'02), pp. 122–130.

Campbell, J. D. 2002b. Characteristics of Group Development of Diagrams. In: Proceedings of the 11th IEEE International Workshops on Enabling Technologies: Infrastructure for Collaborative Enterprises (WETICE'02), pp. 29–34.

Campbell, J. D. 2004. Interaction in Collaborative Computer Supported Diagram Development. Computers in Human Behavior Vol. 20, No. 2, pp. 289–310.

Chong, S. T. and M. Sakauchi. 2000. E-CoBROWSE: Co-navigating the Web with Chat-pointers and Add-ins–Problems and Promises. In: Proceedings of the IASTED International Conference on Parallel and Distributed Computing and Systems (ICPDCS'00), Vol. 2, pp. 803–808.

Chuang, B. 2007. Mozilla Networking Preferences. MozillaZine Knowledge Base. https://developer.mozilla.org/en/Mozilla_Networking_Preferences (Accessed: June 23, 2011).

Corbin, J. M. and A. L. Strauss. 2008. Basics of Qualitative Research: Techniques and Procedures for Developing Grounded Theory. 3rd ed. Los Angeles, London, New Delhi: Sage Publications, ISBN 978-0-8039-5940-8.

Coughlan, J., R. D. Macredie, and N. Patel. 2011. Understanding the consumption process through in-branch and e-mortgage service channels: A first-time buyer perspective. International Journal of Bank Marketing Vol. 29, No. 2, pp. 148–167.

Crane, D. and P. McCarthy. 2008. Comet and Reverse Ajax: The Next-Generation Ajax 2.0. Heidelberg: Springer, ISBN 978-1-590-59998-3.

Curtis, B., H. Krasner, and N. Iscoe. 1988. A Field Study of the Software Design Process for Large Systems. Communications of the ACM Vol. 31, No. 11, pp. 1268–1287.

Daft, R. L. and A. Y. Lewin. 1990. Can Organization Studies Begin to Break out of the Normal Science Straitjacket? An Editorial Essay. Organization Science Vol. 1, No. 1, pp. 1–9.

Dekel, U. 2006. A Study of Artifact Creation and Use in Collaborative Object-oriented Software Design. In: Proceedings of the 21st ACM SIGPLAN Conference on Object Oriented Programming Systems, Languages, and Applications (OOPSLA'06), pp. 748–749.

Dennis, A. R., R. M. Fuller, and J. S. Valacich. 2008. Media, Tasks, and Communication Processes: A Theory of Media Synchronicity. MIS Quarterly Vol. 32, No. 3, pp. 575–600.

Denoue, L., J. Adcock, S. Carter, and G. Golovchinsky. 2009. WebNC: Efficient Sharing of Web Applications. In: Proceedings of the 20th ACM Conference on Hypertext and Hypermedia (HT'09), pp. 365–366.

Dix, A. 1997. Challenges for Cooperative Work on the Web: An Analytical Approach. Computer Supported Cooperative Work (CSCW) Vol. 6, No. 2, pp. 135–156.

Dix, A. 1998. Human-Computer Interaction. 2nd ed. London, New York: Prentice Hall Europe, ISBN 978-0-13-239864-0.

Döbler, T. 2007. Kooperation und Kollaboration mit Web 2.0. i-com - Zeitschrift für interaktive und kooperative Medien Vol. 6, No. 1, pp. 9–13.

Doyle, B., M. Simpson, B. Hoffman, and E. Higdon. 2011. Affluent Investors Seek Online Collaboration—Smart Full-service Firms Will Use The Web To Connect Advisors And Clients. Trends. Forrester Research. http://www.forrester.com/rb/Research/q/id/58443/t/2 (Accessed: June 20, 2011).

Dyck, J., C. Gutwin, S. Subramanian, and C. Fedak. 2004. High-performance telepointers. In: Proceedings of the 2004 ACMConference on Computer Supported Cooperative Work (CSCW'04), pp. 172–181.

East, E. W., J. G. Kirby, and G. Perez. 2004. Improved Design Review through Web Collaboration. Journal of Management in Engineering Vol. 20, No. 2, pp. 51–55.

Esenther, A. W. 2002a. Instant Co-browsing: Lightweight Real-time Collaborative Web Browsing. In: Proceedings of the 11th International Conference of Wold Wide Web (WWW'02), pp. 107–114.

Esenther, A. W. 2002b. Collaborative Web Browsing. Patent US 2002/0138624 Al, issued September 26, 2002.

Fettke, P., C. Houy, and P. Loos. 2010. On the Relevance of Design Knowledge for Design-oriented Business and Information Systems Engineering. Business & Information Systems Engineering Vol. 2, No. 6, pp. 347–358.

Fielding, R., J. Gettys, J. Mogul, H. Frystyk, L. Masinter, P. Leach, and T. Berners-Lee. 1999. HyperText Transfer Protocol—HTTP/1.1. IETF. http://www.ietf.org/rfc/rfc2616.txt (Accessed: June 25, 2010).

Flanagan, D. 2005. Java in a Nutshell. 5th ed. Beijing, Cambridge: O'Reilly Media, ISBN 978-0-596-00773-7.

Fraenkel, M. L. and Singhal, S. K. 2000. Method and System for Portably Enabling View Synchronization over the World-wide Web Using Frame Hierarchies. Patent 6,151,622, issued November 21, 2000.

Frambach, R. T., H. C. A. Roest, and T. V. Krishnan. 2007. The impact of consumer Internet experience on channel preference and usage intentions across the different stages of the buying process. Journal of Interactive Marketing Vol. 21, No. 2, pp. 26–41.

French, A. and P. Layzell. 1998. A Study of Communication and Cooperation in Distributed Software Project Teams. In: Proceedings of the 14th IEEE International Conference on Software Maintenance (ICSM'98), pp. 146–154.

Geisser, M., A. Heinzl, T. Hildenbrand, and F. Rothlauf. 2007. Verteiltes, Internetbasiertes Requirements-Engineering. Wirtschaftsinformatik Vol. 49, No. 3, pp. 199–207.

Giguère, E. 2000. Java 2: Micro Edition. Professional Developer's Guide Serises. New York, Chichester: John Wiley & Sons, ISBN 978-0-471-39065-7.

Graham, C. 1997. Groupscape: Integrating Synchronous Groupware and the World Wide Web. In: Proceedings of the IFIP TC13 International Conference on Human-Computer Interaction (INTERACT'97), pp. 547–554.

Graves, S. J. and C. M. Desai. 2006. Instruction via Chat Reference: Does Co-browse Help? Reference Services Review Vol. 34, No. 3, pp. 340–357.

Greenberg, S. and D. Marwood. 1994. Real Time Groupware as a Distributed System: Concurrency Control and its Effect on the Interface. In: Proceedings of the 1994 ACM Conference on Computer Supported Cooperative Work (CSCW'94), pp. 207–217.

Grönroos, C. 1984. A Service Quality Model and its Marketing Implications. European Journal of Marketing Vol. 18, No. 4, pp. 36–44.

Gutwin, C. and S. Greenberg. 2002. A Descriptive Framework of Workspace Awareness for Real-time Groupware. Computer Supported Cooperative Work (CSCW) Vol. 11, No. 3, pp. 411–446.

Heinrich, L. J., A. Heinzl, and R. Riedl. 2010. Wirtschaftsinformatik: Einführung und Grundlegung. Springer-Lehrbuch. Heidelberg: Springer, ISBN 978-3-642-15425-6.

Hevner, A. R. and S. Chatterjee. 2010. Design Science Research in Information Systems. R. Sharda and S. Voß (Eds.). Integrated Series in Information Systems 22. New York, Heidelberg, London: Springer, ISBN 978-1-4419-5653-8.

Hevner, A. R., S. T. March, J. Park, and S. Ram. 2004. Design Science in Information Systems Research. MIS Quarterly Vol. 28, No. 1, pp. 75–105.

Hill, C., R. Yates, C. Jones, and S. L. Kogan. 2006. Beyond Predictable Workflows: Enhancing Productivity in Artful Business Processes. IBM Systems Journal Vol. 45, No. 4, pp. 663–682.

von Hippel, E. 1988. The Sources of Innovation. New York: Oxford University Press, ISBN 978-0-19-504085-2.

Hong, J. I., J. Heer, S. Waterson, and J. A. Landay. 2001. Webquilt: A Proxy-based Approach to Remote Web Usability Testing. ACM Transactions on Information Systems (TOIS) Vol. 19, pp. 263–285.

Hsieh, M. D., T. P. Wang, C. S. Tsai, and C. C. Tseng. 2006. Stateful Session Handoff for Mobile WWW. Information Sciences Vol. 176, No. 9, pp. 1241–1265.

Hu, J. C., I. Pyarali, and D. C. Schmidt. 1997. Measuring the Impact of Event Dispatching and Concurrency Models on Web Server Performance Over High-speed Networks. In: Proceedings of the IEEE Global Telecommunications Conference (GLOBECOM'97), pp. 1924–1931.

Hutchins, B. 2008. MooTools 1.2 Comet. Google Project Hosting. http://code.google.com/p/moo-comet/ (Accessed: July 20, 2010).

Ichimura, S. and Y. Matsushita. 2005. Lightweight Desktop-sharing System for Web Browsers. In: Proceedings of the IEEE International Conference on Information Technology and Applications (ICITA'05), Vol. 2, pp. 136–141.

IETF. 2011. Principles of the Same-origin Policy. Internet-Draft. Internet Engineering Task Force (IETF). http://tools.ietf.org/id/draft-abarth-principles-of-origin-00.txt (Accessed: June 23, 2011).

Jacobs, S., M. Gebhardt, S. Kethers, and W. Rzasa. 1996. Filling HTML Forms Simultaneously: Coweb—Architecture and Functionality. Computer Networks and ISDN Systems Vol. 28, No. 7-11, pp. 1385–1395.

Jacobson, I., G. Booch, and J. Rumbaugh. 2003. The Unified Software Development Process. Boston: Addison-Wesley, ISBN 978-0-201-57169-1.

Jensen, S., A. Møller, and P. Thiemann. 2009. Type Analysis for Java Script. In: Static Analysis, Vol. 5673, pp. 238–255. Lecture Notes in Computer Science. Berlin, Heidelberg: Springer, ISBN 978-3-642-03237-0.

Jiang, B., J. Yang, and H. R. Arabnia. 2006. Remote Move-related Operation Awareness in Real-time Internet-based Collaborative Graphics Design Systems. In: Proceedings of the 2006 International Conference on Computer Graphics and Virtual Reality (CGVR'06), pp. 138–146.

Johansen, R., J. Charles, R. Mittman, and P. Saffo. 1988. Groupware: Computer Support for Business Teams. Series in Communication Technology and Society. New York, London: Free Press, Collier Macmillan, ISBN 978-0-02-916491-4.

Johnson, C. A., C. P. Wilson, and S. Meyer. 2005. Rethinking the Significance of Cart Abandonment. Forrester Research. http://www.forrester.com/rb/Research/q/id/37912/t/2?src=42341pdf (Accessed: April 27, 2011).

Jupiter Research. 2008. Relieve the Pain of Shopping Cart Abandonment. Webinar. http://www.atg.com/repositories/ContentCatalog Repository_en/webinars/022708Webinar_ShopCart.pdf (Accessed: February 16, 2010).

Kaiser, G. E., S. E. Dossick, W. Jiang, J. J. Yang, and S. X. Ye. 1998. WWW-based Collaboration Environments with Distributed Tool Services. World Wide Web Vol. 1, No. 1, pp. 3–25.

Karsenty, L. 1999. Cooperative Work and Shared Visual Context: An Empirical Study of Comprehension Problems in Side-by-side and Remote Help Dialogues. Human-Computer Interaction Vol. 14, No. 3, pp. 283–315.

Keukelaere, F. D., S. Bhola, M. Steiner, S. Chari, and S. Yoshihama. 2008. SMash—Secure Component Model for Cross-domain Mashups on Unmodified Browsers. In: Proceeding of the 17th International Conference on World Wide Web (WWW'08), pp. 535–544.

King, A. B. 2000. Compression Methods: GIF vs. JPEG vs. PNG. http://webreference.com/dev/graphics/compress.html (Accessed: June 14, 2011).

Kukar-Kinney, M. and A. G. Close. 2009. The Determinants of Consumers' Online Shopping Cart Abandonment. Journal of the Academy of Marketing Science Vol. 38, No. 2, pp. 240–250.

Leavitt, N. 2009. Anonymization Technology Takes a High Profile. Computer Vol. 42, No. 11, pp. 15–18.

Levy, Y. and T. J. Ellis. 2006. A Systems Approach to Conduct an Effective Literature Review in Support of Information Systems Research. Informing Science: International Journal of an Emerging Transdiscipline Vol. 9, pp. 181–212.

Lieberman, H., N. Van Dyke, and A. Vivacqua. 1999. Let's Browse: A Collaborative Browsing Agent. Knowledge-based Systems Vol. 12, No. 8, pp. 427–431.

Lowet, D. and D. Goergen. 2009. Co-browsing Dynamic Web Pages. In: Proceedings of the 18th International Conference on World Wide Web (WWW'09), pp. 941–950.

Lukosch, S. and T. Schümmer. 2004. Communicating Design Knowledge with Groupware Technology Patterns. In: Groupware: Design, Implementation and Use, G.-J. de Vreede, L. A. Guerrero, and G. M. Raventós (Eds.), Vol. 3198, pp. 223–237. Lecture Notes in Computer Science. Berlin, Heidelberg: Springer, ISBN 978-3-540-74811-3.

Luotonen, A. 1998. Web Proxy Servers. Web Infrastructure Series. Upper Saddle River, NJ, USA: Prentice Hall, ISBN 978-0-13-680612-7.

Mao, Z. and C. Herley. 2010. A Robust Link-translating Proxy Server Mirroring the Whole Web. In: Proceedings of the 2010 ACM Symposium on Applied Computing (SAC'10), pp. 818–825.

Markus, M. L., A. Majchrzak, and L. Gasser. 2002. A Design Theory for Systems that support Emergent Knowledge Processes. MIS Quarterly Vol. 26, No. 3, pp. 179–212.

Mehra, A., J. Grundy, and J. Hosking. 2004. Supporting Collaborative Software Design with a Plug-in, Web Services-based Architecture. In: Workshop on Directions in Software Engineering Environments (ICSE'04), pp. 23–28.

Nichols, D., P. Curtis, M. Dixon, and J. Lamping. 1995. High-latency, Low-bandwidth Windowing in the Jupiter Collaboration System. In: Proceedings of the 8th Annual ACM Symposium on User Interface and Software Technology (UIST'95), pp. 111–120.

Niinimäki, T., A. Piri, C. Lassenius, and M. Paasivaara. 2010. Reflecting the Choice and Usage of Communication Tools in GSD Projects with Media Synchronicity Theory. In: Proceedings of the 5th International Conference on Global Software Engineering (ICGSE'10), pp. 3–12.

O'Reilly, T. 2005. What is Web 2.0: Design Patterns and Business Models for the Next Generation of Software. http://oreilly.com/web2/archive/what-is-web-20.html (Accessed: May 7, 2009).

Okoli, C. and K. Schabram. 2010. A Guide to Conducting a Systematic Literature Review of Information Systems Research. Sprouts: Working Papers on Information Systems Vol. 10, No. 26.

Ono, W. 2008. Halley: A Framework for Collaborative Web Applications. CPSC 539W Project. (Working Paper).

Parasuraman, A., V. A. Zeithaml, and L. L. Berry. 1988. SERVQUAL: A Multiple-item Scale for Measuring Consumer Perceptions of Service Quality. Journal of Retailing Vol. 64, No. 1, pp. 12–40.

Pfeffermann, D. and C. R. Rao. 2009. Sample Surveys: Design, Methods and Applications. Amsterdam: Elsevier, ISBN 978-0-444-53124-7.

Pietschmann, S., J. Waltsgott, and K. Meißner. 2010. A Thin-server Runtime Platform for Composite Web Applications. In: Proceedings of the 5th IEEE International Conference on Internet and Web Applications and Services (ICIW'10), pp. 390–395.

Romme, A. G. L. 2003. Making a Difference: Organization as Design. Organization Science Vol. 14, No. 5, pp. 558–573.

Roseman, M. and S. Greenberg. 1996. GroupWeb: A WWW Browser as Real Time Groupware. In: Conference Companion on Human Factors in Computing Systems: Common Ground, pp. 271–272.

Roth, J. and C. Unger. 1998. Dream Team—A Synchronous CSCW Environment for Distance Education. In: Proceedings of the ED-MEDIA/ED-ECOM, Vol. 98, pp. 1185–1190.

Runeson, P. and M. Höst. 2008. Guidelines for Conducting and Reporting Case Study Research in Software Engineering. Empirical Software Engineering Vol. 14, pp. 131–164.

Schreiber, Z., Y. Ghandour, H. Alhalayqa, and S. Shaheen. 2010. System and Method for Browser within a Web Site and Proxy Server. Patent US 2010/0064234 A12010.

Schulze, T., C. Thum, and M. Klems. 2010. Towards Providing Lightweight Access to Legacy Applications as Cloud-based Services. In: Proceedings of the 21st Australasian Conference on Information Systems (ACIS'10).

Schümmer, J. and C. Schuckmann. 2000. COAST—Ein Anwendungsframework für Synchrone Groupware. In: Proceedings of the Net.ObjectDays 2000.

Schümmer, T. and S. Lukosch. 2007. Patterns for Computer-mediated Interaction. Wiley Software Patterns Series. Chichester, UK: John Wiley & Sons, ISBN 978-0-470-02561-1.

Seemann, M. 2007. Dojo Toolkit. schnell + kompakt. Frankfurt: entwickler.press - Software & Support Verlag GmbH, ISBN 978-3-939084-49-5.

Sengupta, B., S. Chandra, and V. Sinha. 2006. A Research Agenda for Distributed Software Development. In: Proceedings of the 28th International Conference on Software Engineering (ICSE'06), pp. 731–740.

Shaw, M. 2002. What Makes Good Research in Software Engineering? International Journal on Software Tools for Technology Transfer Vol. 4, No. 1, pp. 1–7.

Shaw, M. 2003. Writing Good Software Engineering Research Papers. In: Proceedings of the 25th International Conference on Software Engineering (ICSE'03), pp. 726–736.

Souders, S. 2009. Even Faster Web Sites: Performance Best Practices for Web Developers. M. E. Treseler (Ed.). Beijing, Cambridge: O'Reilly Media, ISBN 978-0-596-52230-8.

Stefik, M., D. G. Bobrow, G. Foster, S. Lanning, and D. Tatar. 1987. WYSIWIS Revised: Early Experiences with Multiuser Interfaces. ACM Transactions on Office Information Systems Vol. 5, No. 2, pp. 147–167.

Sun, C. and D. Chen. 2002. Consistency Maintenance in Real-time Collaborative Graphics Editing Systems. ACM Transactions on Computer-Human Interaction Vol. 9, No. 1, pp. 1–41.

Teufel, S., C. Sauter, T. Mühlherr, and K. Bauknecht. 1995. Computerunterstützung für die Gruppenarbeit. Bonn: Addison-Wesley, ISBN 3-89319-878-4.

Theling, T. and P. Loos. 2004. Determinanten und Formen von Unternehmenskooperationen. Information Systems & Management (Working Paper).

Thomson, A. M. and J. L. Perry. 2006. Collaboration Processes: Inside the Black Box. Public Administration Review Vol. 66, No. 1, pp. 20–32.

Thum, C., M. Schwind, and M. Schader. 2009. SLIM—A Lightweight Environment for Synchronous Collaborative Modeling. In: Model Driven Engineering Languages and Systems, pp. 137–151. Lecture Notes in Computer Science. Heidelberg: Springer, ISBN 978-3-642-04424-3.

Tietze, D. A. and J. Rubart. 2001. Dyce: A Framework for Component-based Groupware. Dissertation.

Torraco, R. J. 2005. Writing Integrative Literature Reviews: Guidelines and Examples. Human Resource Development Review Vol. 4, No. 3, pp. 356–367.

Tse, E., J. Histon, S. D. Scott, and S. Greenberg. 2004. Avoiding Interference: How People Use Spatial Separation and Partitioning in SDG Workspaces. In: Proceedings of the 2004 ACM Conference on Computer Supported Cooperative Work (CSCW'04), pp. 252–261.

van Velsen, L. S., M. F. Steehouder, and M. D. T. de Jong. 2007. Evaluation of User Support: Factors That Affect User Satisfaction with Helpdesks and Helplines. Professional Communication, IEEE Transactions on Vol. 50, No. 3, pp. 219–231.

Vroomen, B., B. Donkers, P. C. Verhoef, and P. H. Franses. 2005. Selecting Profitable Customers for Complex Services on the Internet. Journal of Service Research Vol. 8, No. 1, pp. 37 –47.

W3C. 2000. Document Object Model (DOM) Level 2 Events Specification. W3C Recommendation. W3C. http://www.w3.org/TR/DOM-Level-2-Events/ (Accessed: June 8, 2011).

W3C. 2004. Document Object Model (DOM) Specifications. Technical Report. W3C. http://www.w3.org/DOM/DOMTR (Accessed: May 5, 2011).

W3C. 2011. Browser Statistics - Web Statistics and Trends. Higher Screen Resolutions. http://www.w3schools.com/browsers/browsers_resolution_higher.asp (Accessed: June 14, 2011).

Wang, F., C. Rabsch, and P. Liu. 2008. Native Web Browser Enabled SVG-based Collaborative Multimedia Annotation for Medical Images. In: Proceedings of the 24th IEEE International Conference on Data Engineering (ICDE'03), pp. 1219–1228.

Webster, J. and R. T. Watson. 2002. Analyzing the Past to Prepare for the Future: Writing a Literature Review. MIS Quarterly Vol. 26, No. 2, pp. 13–23.

Webster, M. 2005. The Requirements for Managing the Geographically Distributed Development Organization and the CollabNet Solution. IDC. http://www.collab.net/news/library/analystreports.html (Accessed: June 7, 2010).

WHATWG. 2011. Dynamic Script Execution Order. WHATWG Wiki. http://wiki.whatwg.org/wiki/Dynamic_Script_Execution_Order (Accessed: September 23, 2011).

Whitehead, J. 2007. Collaboration in Software Engineering: A Roadmap. In: Future of Software Engineering (FOSE'07), pp. 214–225.

Wilkins, G. 2008. Jetty Continuations. http://docs.codehaus.org/display/JETTY/Continuations (Accessed: July 4, 2010).

Wiltse, H. and J. Nichols. 2009. PlayByPlay: Collaborative Web Browsing for Desktop and Mobile Devices. In: Proceedings of the 27th International Conference on Human Factors in Computing Systems, pp. 1781–1790.

Winter, R. 2008. Interview with Alan R. Hevner on Design Science. Business & Information Systems Engineering Vol. 1, No. 1, pp. 126–129.

Young, G. O., E. G. Brown, T. J. Keitt, J. K. Owyang, R. Koplowitz, and H. Shey. 2008. Global Enterprise Web 2.0 Market Forecast:

2007 to 2013. Forrester Research. http://www.forrester.com/rb/Research/q/id/43850/t/2 (Accessed: January 17, 2010).

Yue, C., Z. Chu, and H. Wang. 2009. RCB: A Simple and Practical Framework for Real-time Collaborative Browsing. In: Proceedings of the 2009 USENIX Annual Technical Conference (USENIX'09), pp. 29–43.

Zammetti, F. W. 2006. Practical Ajax Projects with Java Technology. C. Mills (Ed.). New York: Springer, ISBN 978-1-59059-695-1.

Zammetti, F. W. 2008. Practical Dojo Projects. S. Anglin (Ed.). New York: Springer, ISBN 978-1-4302-1066-5.

Zhu, L., I. Benbasat, and Z. Jiang. 2010. Let's Shop Online Together: An Empirical Investigation of Collaborative Online Shopping Support. Information Systems Research Vol. 21, No. 4, pp. 872–891.

ENTSCHEIDUNGSUNTERSTÜTZUNG FÜR ÖKONOMISCHE PROBLEME

Herausgegeben von Christian Becker, Wolfgang Gaul, Armin Heinzl, Martin Schader und Daniel Veit

Band 1 Ingo Böckenholt: Mehrdimensionale Skalierung qualitativer Daten. Ein Instrument zur Unterstützung von Marketingentscheidungen. 1989.

Band 2 Jürgen Joseph: Arbeitswissenschaftliche Aspekte der betrieblichen Einführung neuer Technologien am Beispiel von Computer Aided Design (CAD). Felduntersuchung zur Ermittlung arbeitswissenschaftlicher Empfehlungen für die Einführung neuer Technologien. 1990.

Band 3 Eva Schönfelder: Entwicklung eines Verfahrens zur Bewertung von Schichtsystemen nach arbeitswissenschaftlichen Kriterien. 1992.

Band 4 Michael Bargl: Akzeptanz und Effizienz computergestützter Dispositionssysteme in der Transportwirtschaft. Empirische Studien zur Implementierungsforschung von Entscheidungsunterstützungssystemen am Beispiel computergestützter Tourenplanungssysteme. 1994.

Band 5 Reinhold Decker: Analyse und Simulation des Kaufverhaltens auf Konsumgütermärkten. Konzeption eines modell- und wissensorientierten Systems zur Auswertung von Paneldaten. 1994.

Band 6 Wolfgang Gaul / Martin Schader (Hrsg.): Wissensbasierte Marketing-Datenanalyse. Das WIMDAS-Projekt. 1994.

Band 7 Daniel Baier: Konzipierung und Realisierung einer Unterstützung des kombinierten Einsatzes von Methoden bei der Positionierungsanalyse. 1994.

Band 8 Ulrich Lutz: Preispolitik im internationalen Marketing und westeuropäische Integration. 1994.

Band 9 Kirsten Petersen: Design eines Courseware-Entwicklungssystems für den computerunterstützten universitären Unterricht. CULLIS-Teilprojekt I. 1996.

Band 10 Stefan Neumann: Einsatz von Interactive Video im computerunterstützten universitären Unterricht. CULLIS Teilprojekt II. 1996.

Band 11 Eberhard Aust: Simultane Conjointanalyse, Benefitsegmentierung, Produktlinien- und Preisgestaltung. 1996.

Band 12 Peter Heydebreck: Technologische Verflechtung. Ein Instrument zum Erreichen von Produkt- und Prozeßinnovationserfolg. 1996.

Band 13 Michael Pesch: Effiziente Verkaufsplanung im Investitionsgütermarketing. 1997.

Band 14 Frank Wartenberg: Entscheidungsunterstützung im persönlichen Verkauf. 1997.

Band 15 Thomas Lechler: Erfolgsfaktoren des Projektmanagements. 1997.

Band 16 Alexandre Saad: Anbahnung und Erfolg von europäischen kooperativen F&E-Projekten. Eine empirische Analyse anhand von ESPRIT-Projekten. 1998.

Band 17 Michael Löffler: Integrierte Preisoptimierung. 1999.

Band 18 Frank Säuberlich: KDD und Data Mining als Hilfsmittel zur Entscheidungsunterstützung. 2000.

INFORMATIONSTECHNOLOGIE UND ÖKONOMIE

(Neuer Reihentitel ab Band 19)

Band 19 Rainer Kiel: Dialog-gesteuerte Regelsysteme. Definition, Eigenschaften und Anwendungen. 2001.

Band 20 Axel Korthaus: Komponentenbasierte Entwicklung computergestützter betrieblicher Informationssysteme. 2001.

Band 21 Markus Aleksy: Entwicklung einer komponentenbasierten Architektur zur Implementierung paralleler Anwendungen mittels CORBA. Mit Beispielen aus den Wirtschaftswissenschaften. 2003.

Band 22 Michael Zapf: Flexible Kundeninteraktionsprozesse im Communication Center. 2003.

Band 23 Yvonne Staack: Kundenbindung im eBusiness. Eine kausalanalytische Untersuchung der Determinanten, Dimensionen und Verhaltenskonsequenzen der Kundenbindung im Online-Shopping und Online-Brokerage. 2004.

Band 24 Lars Schmidt-Thieme: Assoziationsregel-Algorithmen für Daten mit komplexer Strutkur. Mit Anwendungen im Web Mining. 2003.

Band 25 Stefan Hocke: Flexibilitätsmanagement in der Logistik. Systemtheoretische Fundierung und Simulation logistischer Gestaltungsparameter. 2004.

Band 26 Viktor Jung: Markteintrittsgestaltung neugegründeter Unternehmen. Situationsspezifische und erfolgsbezogene Analyse. 2004.

Band 27 Lars Brehm: Postimplementierungsphase von ERP-Systemen in Unternehmen. Organisatorische Gestaltung und kritische Erfolgsfaktoren. 2004.

Band 28 Ralf Gitzel: Model-Driven Software Development Using a Metamodel-Based Extension Mechanism for UML. 2006.

Band 29 Bernd Stauß: Optimale Gestaltung von Auswahlmenüs und deren Verwendung im Variantenmanagement. 2006.

Band 30 Nils Schumacher: EDI via XML. Potentiale und Strategien für global orientierte kleine und mittlere Unternehmen. 2007.

Band 31 Christian Cuske: Quantifizierung operationeller Technologierisiken bei Kreditinstituten. Eine Ontologie-zentrierte Vorgehensweise im Spannungsfeld bankinterner und aufsichtsrechtlicher Sichtweise. 2007.

Band 32 Matthias Merz: Konzeptioneller Entwurf und prototypische Implementierung einer Sicherheitsarchitektur für die Java Data Objects-Spezifikation. 2008.

Band 33 Tobias Hildenbrand: Improving Traceability in Distributed Collaborative Software Development. A Design Science Approach. 2008.

Band 34 Karen H. L. Tso-Sutter: Towards Metadata-Aware Algorithms for Recommender Systems. 2010.

Band 35 Thomas Schoberth: Eine Längsschnittstudie der Kommunikationsaktivität in virtuellen Gemeinschaften. 2010.

Band 36 Nima Mazloumi: Entwurf eines Refernzmodells und Frameworks zur Erstellung hybrider Lehr- und Lernszenarien. Mit Fallbeispielen aus der Betriebswirtschaftslehre und der Wirtschaftsinformatik. 2010.

Band 37 Anja Zöller: Effizienzanalyse grundlegender Gestaltungsgrößen der OP-Organisation. 2010.

Band 38 Jessica Katharina Winkler: International Entry Mode Choices of Software Firms. An Analysis of Product-Specific Determinants. 2009.

Band 39 Martin J. Lafleur: *Loyalty Profiling.* Erfolgsdimensionen und Modellansätze eines effizienten und effektiven Customer Relationship Management. 2010.

Band 40 Ingo Ott: Effizientes Prozessmanagement im öffentlichen Dienst. 2010.

Band 41 Stefan Seedorf: Ontologie-gestützte Entwicklung komponentenbasierter Anwendungssysteme. Ein wissensbasiertes Informationssystem zur Unterstützung der Entwicklung und Wartung von Geschäftskomponenten (KompIS). 2010.

Band 42 Dominic Gastes: Erhebungsprozesse und Konsistenzanforderungen im Analytic Hierarchy Process (AHP). 2011.

Band 43 *erscheint in Kürze*

Band 44 Olaf Thiele: Informationsvisualisierungen auf mobilen Endgeräten zur Unterstützung des betrieblichen Datenmanagements. 2011.

Band 45 Krisztian Antal Buza: Fusion Methods for Time-Series Classification. 2011.

Band 46 Thomas Kude: The Coordination of Inter-Organizational Networks in the Enterprise Software Industry. The Perspective of Complementors. 2012.

Band 47 Alexandra Rebecca Klages: Clusteranalyse für Netzwerke. 2012.

Band 48 Christian Thum: Enabling Lightweight Real-time Collaboration. 2012.

FSC
www.fsc.org
MIX
Papier | Fördert
gute Waldnutzung
FSC® C083411

Kolibri 360 GmbH
Ferdinand-Jühlke-Straße 7
99095 Erfurt, Deutschland
produktsicherheit@kolibri360.de